What if...Why not?

WALKING THROUGH THE DOORS OF ADVENTURE

Written by
Kevin E. Beasley

Cameron...
Chase hard after the Maker.
He will fill your life with
hope and adventure!

Ke E Beesly
"Why Not?"
2014

I could never acknowledge in a few lines all of the people who have allowed this to become a reality...

Scott Hunter, Keith Caprara, Larry and Sharon Hale, Kevin and Sonya Yates, and Peter Goodwin, thank you so much for your encouragement and support over the years.

Julie, Grace, Gabe, Daniel and Susana Beasley, thank you for putting up with my time away from home.

Chelsie Stulz, Melanie Patterson, Kim Vantrease, Sonya Yates, Lindsay Devenbeck, and Steven Dixon, thank you for all of your hard work that made this book possible.

And thanks to all those I've journeyed with in the faith for the past twenty-five years. There's nothing on Earth like God's people.

Thanks to my mom and dad who allowed me to be me when it didn't make a lot of sense.

Most of all, thank the Maker and His Son Redeemer for giving me the only thing worth living and dying for!

Join the conversation at http://whynotthebook.com

Find out more about visiting Alaska at http://alaskanventures.com

Adventure

"People are not like numbers. They are more like letters. And letters want to become stories and stories are made to be shared." - Jonathan Safran Foer in <u>Extremely Loud and Incredibly Close</u> (the movie)[1]

I love telling stories.

The only thing better than telling stories is living them. And I have lived no better stories than the ones I have experienced in the Last True Wilderness: Alaska. Therefore, my favorite stories to tell are those I have collected there. One week in Alaska yields a dozen tales, which can be told for years to come; new twists and turns reveal themselves each time I remember an Alaskan adventure.

I have hesitated to put these stories into writing—partly due to laziness and partly because of the amazing Alaskan stories I have read from others over the years. I have only spent a total of eighty-two days, over seven trips, in this virtually untouched wonderland. How captivating can a couple of months worth of stories be when set beside tales of heroism and bravery such as those of Dick Proenneke, who invested a large portion of his life to solitude and study of southwest Alaskan wildlife, weather and wilderness? How could anyone find any return investing time in a journal such as mine after reading of the dangers and adventure of

Christopher McCandless and his untimely death in the early 90s? What heart could be mended any tighter after listening to the tragedy and redemption of Jeremy Davis and his family after the sudden loss of three of their children on a wintry day on Lake Clark a few short years ago? No one!

I have decided to write these stories not to impress readers or compete with those who have gone before and certainly not to compare my stories to their experiences, for I have nothing to compare. I simply write to share— although my experiences may not be life shattering for you, they have made me who I am. If only my family reads them, the tales will have served well.

I am who I am because of a place on the map that opened up my heart to hear. The place did not make me, it simply cracked me wide open so the Maker could shake me and wake me up to the reality of who I am...and more importantly, Who He is.

For that reason I am grateful to the place and more grateful to the Maker. He is the teller of these tales. He is the artist who painted, with both broad strokes and intricate detail, a picture that cannot be fully explained without a journey into the story itself. You have your own work of art...your own story. Whether that masterpiece is a place such as Alaska or a person such as your spouse or best friend, you must explore it in order to truly understand it. It should be mined for the treasure that lies within, and then it must be communicated to be shared.

For those of you who are considering an adventure north, I say do not deprive yourself of what no other place can offer. But whether you are in Alaska or your own backyard...Go! Live. Rest. Breathe.
Alaska is not the only place to escape the trappings of a busy life; there may be other places just as fitting.

My trips are not unique; they resemble the same journey all of us take throughout life. Yours are no less dramatic than the tales you will read here and no less important. It's the journey into manhood or womanhood, into freedom from bondage, into hope from hopelessness, from independence to interdependence. It is the pathway through the door of hope—it is the place where the spirit of who we will be collides with the reality of who is. Are these stories singular or plural...yes. It's one journey with many stops along the way.

Frederick Buechner in his memoir, Telling Secrets says, *"My story is important not because it is mine, God knows, but because if I tell it anything like right, the chances are you will recognize that in many ways it is also yours."*[2] That's how I feel about these stories—and that's why I write them.

So, journey with me through simple stories that have made me a more simple man. Consider the lessons the Maker has shared with me through these journeys and see if He has something for you. Keep your heart open and your awareness keen; it is not I who tells tales that can melt a frozen heart, it is He. He may choose to use one of these simple stories and He may not. They are just my feeble offering in response to the wonderful gift He has given me...ADVENTURE!

Alaska or Bust!

"Life is either a daring adventure or nothing. To keep our faces toward change and behave like free spirits in the presence of fate is strength undefeatable." - Helen Keller[3]

Adventure is about what we do; not what we plan, strategize or dream about. Adventure begins with "what ifs" and "why nots."

"What if I were to step out to chase that dream?"

"Why not take the first steps and see what happens?"

When we step through the doorway of adventure our life is suddenly worth the living. And we experience life as it was meant to be. But every journey starts with a first step. And my first shaky step was as a young starry-eyed college student.

Every young man feels deep within himself a longing for more. It hovers around his heart like a nagging housefly. It is that elusive fulfillment which he can't seem to apprehend. This familiar feeling is particularly vocal in early adulthood when almost every major life decision is screaming for an answer to the looming questions of life. How am I going to spend the rest of my days? Who will be the woman I marry? What career should I pursue? Will I be able to make a difference? Will my life have any meaning? Significance is the moving target for which a young man's wavering arrow is aimed and he doubts whether he has the accuracy and range to hit its mark. "Do I have what it takes?" he asks himself. That's where I found myself in the winter of 1996.

There are only a few times from our first breath to our last that a short sentence will change the course of forever.

"I'm going to Alaska and I think you are supposed to go with me," Scott said with a stark air of confidence.

This pivotal moment in my life occurred about a week into a fifteen-day period set aside for spiritual focus. Three young men and I were meeting together to pray and listen for spiritual direction that would direct our young stallion hearts toward the life we were meant to live.

We were pursuing bachelor's degrees in a quaint university in north Alabama, but we were restless: anxious to change the world and hungry to experience significance and adventure. The kind of adventure a young man thinks only comes from fighting battles and courting maidens. Confused about our identity and passionate about our faith, we were looking for meaning and purpose; longing for the adventure that would propel us into the rest of our lives; waiting for it to be revealed and walking shoulder to shoulder hoping it would come within this two-week experiment.

The four of us found ourselves wrestling with these questions and hoping for some direction as we gathered in the little three-bedroom apartment. For at least two hours each night we sat in silence and asked the Maker for a clue to the rest of our lives. Fifteen days of fasting and praying in that little college apartment: the hours passed in quietness to the human ear, but as time moved on, the four of us realized that a deafening roar was shaking the core of our hearts. As it raged, it began to change our lives and hearts much like a natural disaster would redirect the course of a raging river and lead it down another path.

My path would eventually be directed to leave that little university with only a couple semesters left in my college career to start afresh in a Bible college in central Florida. It took about a year's journey to arrive on that little campus and it set me back several semesters in my course of studies, but in reality, it was the shortest path to my intended future.

Jeromy's river would weave its way to a summer mission experience that would lead him to a new direction in life. Ken's path eventually meandered to Nashville to toy with a career in the music industry and then into sales. And Scott's river would take him and two others, myself included, to a place and experience that would have an unfolding purpose for the rest of our lives.

"I'm going to Alaska and I think you are supposed to go with me."

"What are you talking about, man?" I said on the outside, while inside I thought he had lost his mind. Never in my life had I felt compelled to go to Alaska.

"I'm supposed to go to Alaska," he said with the confidence of a crouching lion ready to pounce upon his next meal.

"When do you think you are supposed to go to Alaska?" we asked curiously.

"This summer. Are you going with me?"

It was barely a question. It rang out more like a directive, as if Scott had heard from the Maker that we were to go and he was simply announcing his revelation. And that is how this all began.

It was not just the beginning of a story, but the beginning of dozens: a simple invitation from a boy who had heard the voice of the Maker and who simply responded. As if the officer of the watch barked out orders to the helmsman, "Hard Right Rudder," and the faithful sailor blindly obliged. That sudden change of course was the shift I needed to open the doorway into the richness of living a life of adventure and passion. As the far-fetched fairy tale became a reality, my eyes were opened to the adventure of life lived radically following the voice of the Maker of all creation. I reluctantly agreed to follow. It felt something like the fishermen must have felt when they were standing by their boats tending to the family business and the Redeemer swaggered over to them and said, "Follow me, I will make you fishers of men."

I couldn't resist the persistent voice of both Scott and the Maker. Turning my back on reason and asking "why not," I began preparing for the first of what would become many trips to a place where the problems and distractions of life cannot follow. Alaska!

Best Laid Plans

The details of that first trip to Alaska would be tested, tried, and tweaked up to the day we climbed into the 1986 Ford Bronco, which ironically carried the license plate number 25ARK02. We engaged the engine and set sail in our four-wheeled rescue boat, as it delivered us from the dangers of the mundane. Our destination was Wasilla, Alaska, about forty miles north of Anchorage. Our journey would take us from church to church to host youth events in Kentucky, Missouri and Colorado. We would cross the U.S. border into Canada from Montana and arrive at our destination six days after our departure.

As Scott shared his story with friends and family, everyone seemed to want to journey with us. A month into the planning process we had twelve college students ready to hop into a van and go. A church in Florence, Alabama, had committed a fifteen-passenger van and it looked like nothing stood in the way of a dozen passionate students taking off on a summer "missions trip." As these twelve students began to tell their parents the exciting news, the students' zeal for adventure yielded to the authority of their parents' fear of danger. They dropped out one by one, most due to parental concern and others from fear of the journey. Looking back today as a parent of four, I would expect nothing less. In the end there were three of us…Scott, Kevin and Keith.

I can only guess how many times I wanted to relent. My timid mind was tucking tail and crying out for mercy. I was not convinced that this trip was possible nor was I sold on the fact that it was wise. With the 20/20 nature of hindsight, it may have, in fact, been neither, and that was the beauty of it; it was a blind leap of faith. Each time one of the phone calls came in from another friend, who could not go for this reason or that, I would waver. Walking a tightrope, each step of the way I had to regain balance and only hope for stability. To be honest, I cannot remember telling my parents about the trip. I can only imagine what they must have said. But, my parents knew that Scott and I had taken these kinds of risks before in our fourteen-year friendship and that once we had made up our minds we were as good as gone. Somehow I was with Scott when the ARK02 set sail on the long journey. I am forever grateful I was; it changed my life forever.

The Three Gypsies

Scott and I were the only two from the original group

of four from the college apartment experiment who were able to make the trip. As we moved closer to our departure date we began to feel more and more like gypsies preparing for a journey through an unknown land with only the bare essentials in tow.

Myself? I was a misfit from a small town...or at least that was how I felt. It's not that I thought I was better than anyone, I just felt like a stranger. Perhaps it had to do with my broken family life at the age of twelve or my insecurity in the things of boyhood, such as sports and girls. No matter the reason, I just felt out of place my whole life. Even in college I didn't know where or with whom to hang out. I needed an identity. At the age of fifteen I thought I found it in church, but even there I was misunderstood and isolated within two years. This led to social and emotional independence that would be tested time and again throughout my life.

Scott strikes those who know him as a man of conviction and passion. We had been in a close friendship since third grade. As long-term friendships go, we were often the best of buddies and occasionally mere acquaintances, but never either for a long period of time. Our Alaskan adventure changed that. Since our return home in 1996, we have been as close as the closest brothers. He and his wife and children live next door to us even now and we see each other several times a week. We will never know if it was this journey that bonded us so closely, but I suspect it played a huge role in our life-long friendship. Scott has returned many times to Alaska...the place where it all began. He even moved there for a short period early in his marriage. The rigors and cost of life in Alaska was more than they were prepared for, so they soon returned to civilization, but their experience was invaluable.

As we prepared for the trip we picked up a third restless wanderer. Keith was a fellow student at our university and the one other person who was able to chase his curiosity all the way to Alaska. We did not know Keith that well. We knew he was quirky. We realized he was out of his comfort zone pursuing risk and adventure. We understood his level of discomfort with the outdoors and his fear of wild animals. What we loved was his heart. None of us are perfect and we all have unhealthy motives in the deep recesses of our hearts, but as far as we could tell, Keith was the real deal. He loved the Maker and he was meant to travel this journey.

I still don't know what Keith must have been searching for. Nor do I understand his willingness to step into this place of discomfort. But Keith was ready...sitting on the starting line waiting for the gun to fire with the anticipation of a sprinter competing in his first Olympic event. I am so proud of Keith. I am so proud of anyone who overcomes fear in order to follow the Maker with absolute abandon. We rarely see one another these days, but when we do it is as if we could look across a crowded room, meet eyes and write a novel together without ever speaking a word. There are experiences in life after which you know another in ways that a thousand words cannot communicate.

Most of the events of the rest of my life can be attributed in some way to these three weeks at the age of twenty-two. It was more than a turning point. It was a necessary journey that I was supernaturally compelled to take. The drive itself was not a 9,774-mile transport on wheels, it was a life-long trip in which my destination has not been reached and will not be until the day I lay my head in its final resting place. The view from the window of life gets better by the day. The journey from what was to what will be holds more adventure than a mind can imagine. I look forward to the final mile, but will enjoy the scenery as long as I travel.

Upon our arrival back in north Alabama twelve days and many miles later, these three men would be more than friends. We would be a band of gypsies who found connectedness in a shared adventure. None of us would ever be the same.

In recent years, I have come to know these types of experiences as liminal space. Liminality is the state between what was and what is to come. It is a place of transition where the old "normal" transitions to a new "normal." Arnold Van Gennep and Victor Turner first defined liminal space in relation to ritualistic rites of passage in tribal communities. Liminality is known as the space "betwixt and between." In this space in the middle, social norms are minimized and people are on equal ground without regard to social hierarchies or categorizations. On the other side of the liminal experience, those journeying together experience a new level of relationship beyond community. This relationship is referred to as communitas and is only accessible through a liminal experience. The relationship between the three of us can only be explained by the shared journey when life was put on hold in order to experience an adventure through danger and discomfort, along with the joys of laughter and success.

The experiences we had together cannot be described with enough detail to allow people to understand the full impact it had on our lives. In the following pages, I will offer them from my perspective and hope to give you a taste of the joys we experienced. Then I can only hope that you choose to take your own journey. The destination is irrelevant. Whether it's Alaska or just down the road to help clean up after a

14

natural disaster, may you experience the excitement of the journey we felt as we followed our own "what ifs" and "why nots."

The months following the week in the little apartment and leading up to the departure were filled with planning and dreaming, details and disappointment, but the excitement of the adventure overshadowed it all. I took care of the route and stops while Scott handled the funds and networking. We were full of life and void of doubt. We were bound for Alaska and there was no looking back. All the questions about the future that were staring us in the face just a few weeks prior, were set aside to make room for the adventure ahead. It would lead to unknown destinations and new relationships that would change us, as we were a part of changing those we encountered. The liminal space would transport us to another side of our experience of life, both personally and as a group, and only the Maker knew what that would look and feel like.

The Three Gypsies and ARK02
Somewhere Along the Alaska Highway

The Ark of the Pavement

"Life is what happens to you while you're busy making other plans." - John Lennon[4]

"Accept the things to which fate binds you, and love the people with whom fate brings you together, but do so with all your heart." - Marcus Aurelius, Meditations

The ARK02 was her name and transportation was her game.

With well over 200,000 miles and a decade of road experience, she was our only hope to Alaska. As several options for transportation fell through the cracks, it dawned upon Scott that the ARK02 would set sail to Wasilla, on that scorching hot day in May 1996. We had no idea what we were about to put her through and how courageous she would face it—it was only the Maker who would empower her to finish the course.

We were three and a half days into our journey with two youth services behind us: the first in a little First Baptist church in a small rural town called Hebron, Kentucky, and the second in a St. Louis, Missouri, inner city mission called Compton Heights. They were two totally different cultures and two vastly different experiences. We left St. Louis late for an overnight drive

17

to Monument, Colorado, with me at the wheel, Scott in the passenger seat and Keith in our makeshift sleeping quarters in the back of the burgundy rescue boat. Our gear and supplies were secured with care on the top of the ARK02 in a spider web of bungees. I was in for a long night as the other two passengers were resting up for the day ahead.

I'll never forget the loneliness of the straight, flat roads of central Kansas. I am pretty sure I was able to get in several naps at the wheel without even knowing it as the drone of the engine kept me in a half-sleep for most of the night; it was the Maker who kept us between the ditches. I was determined to arrive at our destination in plenty of time to prepare for our largest youth event of the trip the next evening. When necessary, I would stop for gas or a dose of caffeine to get me through the next hour. On one stop, I made a quick call to the girl whose memory and mystery kept my mind active enough to continue the drive—I was already homesick. There's nothing that will sooth a young man's longing for home more than thoughts of the girl that almost kept him there. I had been away from home many times before, but not with the prospect of the danger that lie ahead. The fear made me want to return to safety. I almost turned the truck around several times to head for home. The feelings intensified when my "rescuer" could not talk on the phone because she was sleeping.

Not long after the sun crested over the flat vista ahead and we passed the long awaited beacon of hope that announced we had arrived to "Colorful Colorado," the sleeping gypsies awoke from their slumber. Somewhere along the way we shifted seats in our musical chairs game of drive, ride, sleep.

Scott began to veer right following a sign that read: "Exit 359: Limon, Colorado." My assumption was a quick stop for fuel and then the excitement of seeing the Great Rocky Mountains rising up in all their majesty over the western horizon. Instead I looked out the window at a sandy field full of lanky cattle, in the rear view mirror for a backwards view of I-70 and then over to Scott who was calmly proclaiming that something was wrong. It seemed the ARK02 was sick.

"No way," I exclaimed. Three days in and our hope had already sprung a leak.

Scott was right; she was done for the day. Cell phones were still a thing of the future and I have no idea who took a walk that afternoon, (my educated guess says Scott), but the welcome arrival of yet another rescue boat came not a moment too soon. This rescuer was a truck with a hook on the back and a sign on his side reading "George's Repair Shop." We took a ride in that truck with the ARK02 and all our belongings riding behind in a parade of sunken hope through the middle of small town America. We were taken straight to George's for a long afternoon as we wondered how we would arrive at our destination a couple hours away in time to fulfill our missional duties.

Sometimes I forget that there's a time to surrender and re-arrange plans. To this day I struggle with that simple fact of life. I took to heart the humanistic proverb "where there's a will, there's a way" as I grew into a young man. I probably should have let it go, but I couldn't. We would arrive at Monument Hill Church in time to prepare for the event; I felt that we made a commitment and we would be a failure if we did not follow through. Looking back and being delivered from APPS (acute people pleasing syndrome), I now realize that this problem was more about my fear of failure than it was about the Maker's plan for the night. Nevertheless, if I were to go down, it would be kicking and screaming…and screaming I was!

22

We had encountered our first stumbling block on our Journey into "what ifs" and "why nots" and I would learn a lesson that I would carry for the rest of my life.

If I remember anything on that massive road trip, it is a conversation that occurred in the waiting room of that old greasy garage. I was in a panic, determined to get us to our destination on time. After the fourth or fifth time I asked the mechanic if he would be done on time, he looked at me and spoke those dreaded words that sent me into a state of despair, "We're going to have to keep her overnight."

"What?" I said. I was thinking almost out loud. *How could this be? This cannot be the will of God!* I looked gravely at the mechanic and proclaimed, "You have made a mistake!" But the unavoidable reality was that the job was too big to finish in a half day.

I was pacing the waiting room trying to figure out what I was going to do to fix this mess. My willful flesh reared its ugly head as it often does and refused to bow to this perceived state of defeat. Scott came over and laid his hand on my back and said, "Kevin, let's pray."

Let me preface this sentence by saying that it really happened as much as I wish it had not, "I DON'T HAVE TIME TO PRAY!" It was intense and it was loud. My best friend of many years before, and even longer after, forced me to a seat and into a state of consciousness that the Maker still cared.

After a few sentences of asking Him for direction, I was sure I heard His voice. It was small and it was quiet, but it was firm. "Go make a phone call."

"A phone call? Who will I call?" I asked.

"Just go make a phone call." The Maker spoke as clearly as if He were one of the travelers sitting beside me.

I bounded into the office of the mechanic and asked the attendant for a phone book. I looked at her intently and patiently asked, "If you were going to call a church for help, who would you call?"

She said with confident resolve, "You can call whoever you want to call, but just don't call this one." She took her greasy finger and pointed to a listing that read, "First American Baptist Church of Limon, Colorado."

I knew as quickly as her words drifted past her smoke-stained teeth that I was bound to call the First American Baptist Church of Limon, Colorado. She asked me if I was sure about that and I assured her I was, so she dialed the number and passed the receiver to me while shaking her head in doubt. I was ready for whatever the apparent monster on the other end could dish out.

"Hello?" a voice said at the other end.

"Hi, is this the pastor?"

"I guess you could say that."

"Well, this may sound weird, but I am with two other guys and we are on a missions trip from Alabama and we are headed to Alaska. Our car is broken down and we were wondering if you would be willing to help us out. We need to get to Colorado Springs by 4 p.m."

"WHAT...a mission trip? I can't help you boys, missions is against my religion."

I was beginning to realize what the lady with the smoke-stained teeth was trying to tell me.

"Okay, thank you anyway." As the receiver slipped away from my ear and made its way toward its better half, I heard a roar of laughter emanating through the earpiece.

"Ha, ha, ha, ha...I'm just kiddin. Where are you?" he asked.

"We're at George's Garage."

"I'll be there in a jiff."

As I hung up the phone I looked at smoke-stained lady and smiled.

"Good luck to you," she said.

I ran to share the good news with the other gypsies and we marveled at how the Maker works and I began to realize that these battles are not ours to fight. We simply ask Him for what's next and humbly obey. He'll do the rest.

Fifteen minutes passed and I wondered if American Baptist Pastor had set us up for disappointment. Just as I was considering a second call, a small, smoky gray, foreign four-door car came screeching into the parking lot and did a donut right in front of the shop doors of the garage.

The driver side door flew open and a man shouted at the top of his lungs, "Come on boys, I got the Methodist preacher's car and we gonna get you to the Springs."

American Baptist Pastor was a big man; I would guess about two hundred eighty pounds with a face full of hair. We jumped in for some unknown and unexplainable reason; some call it blind faith and others call it stupidity. The car spun out with the front wheels screaming as we began our journey in our third rescue boat of the trip in as many days.

I was saddled up in the front seat and Scott and Keith were in the back. With time to kill and purpose in our heart, we began to question American Baptist Pastor. He began to share a story way too common among the working class pastor or any church pastor for that matter—he just could not do enough to make them happy; he just could not perform up to their standards; he just could not make it much longer in this environment—he just needed a change. As we shared our story of the fifteen-day spiritual focus and the Maker's voice and how He directed us on this journey, American Baptist Pastor began to get tears in his eyes. "You think you needed me, but I really needed you today," he said through his tears. "Thank you for being obedient."

Whether it's religious leadership or feeding the poor, teaching children English or repairing teeth overseas, it's ironically the most meaningful things in life that offer little financial reward. There are usually three reasons why folks choose to spend their lives on things that have little return. The first is to fulfill a generational lineage. Children see what drives their parents and why they do what they do. This often plants small seeds of passion in them and they feel obligated to follow.

The second is a response to some area of brokenness in a person's life. When deep needs go unmet in a person, there arises an unquenchable desire to have those needs met. When it is affirmation that was withheld, for example, the need for affirmation causes a mind and heart to wander around looking for it until it finds it. One of the best places to be affirmed is in a place where one is doing "good deeds." "Oh, isn't Johnny wonderful," says Aunt Martha, "he has given his whole life away to serve the poor in Africa." When Johnny senses that kind of affirmation, he works harder at becoming better at serving the poor. So his paycheck becomes the affirmation that will relinquish his heart of a desire for financial return. He finds what he's always been looking for.

The third is that they have been changed by some tangible or intangible experience and they have a crossroads moment where they commit to return a portion of what they have received back to random people in random places. When someone's life is

26

revolutionized, they want nothing less than to be part of the revolution, and that often looks like dedicating their lives to some pursuit related to the movement that impacted them. Some church experience radically transforms Johnny's life and allows him to see the Maker for who He is, the Redeemer. The Maker takes the mess of Johnny's life and redeems it into something beautiful to experience and Johnny's only fulfilling response is to dedicate his life in service to the Maker. Because he was impacted in church, he deduces that he should give his life to the church.

I most respect the latter of these three. Not that the other two are not honorable and fruitful, but the third is most raw and sincere. The problem is that the person never realizes until he is several years into serving the church that it wasn't the church that revolutionized his life, but the Maker. And he finds within the church many whose lives haven't been revolutionized and his early experience doesn't match his later one. This causes confusion and disenchantment. The revolutionized leader then begins to think thoughts like, "this is not what I signed up for." He often ends up thinking that his initial revolution was not the real deal and responds in one of two ways: he either leaves his "dream job" for something easier with more return or he settles into a mediocre life of service where nothing ever really changes, but folks are content.

American Baptist Pastor was right in the middle of trying to figure all this out. If I had to guess, I'd bet he was the third option. His life had been radically changed and he had chosen to dedicate all he had to being part of revolutionizing others lives. Now he was facing the un-revolutionized control of his leadership board, and the day-to-day grind of surviving and pleasing the status quo was more than he could bear.

Now he'd come face-to-face with a trio of gypsies who were not settled into the status quo, but living life on the edge of the revolution. This is not a glorification of the gypsies; each of the three at some time in life has settled into half-existence and bowed down to the stronghold of sub-revolutionary contentedness. But at this particular point in life, their passion for revolution collided with American Baptist Pastor's battle with the day-to-day grind of keeping peace. Rarely does keeping peace and fighting for a revolution work together. The big, burly teddy bear in him responded.

American Baptist Pastor made sure we knew as we began our ride to "The Springs" that, as soon as he dropped us off, he had to get the Methodist preacher's car back to Limon and also be on time for an appointment he had later that evening. That was no problem for us; we were just in awe of the help from the Maker.

When we arrived at Monument Hill Baptist Church at four thirty that afternoon, American Baptist Pastor asked if we thought it would be okay for him to stay through the service. Sometimes the promise of adventure takes precedence over pressing commitments. We assured him it was fine.

It was about midnight when we arrived back in that church parking lot from riding the church bus to drop off the youth bussed in from the inner city. We said our final *goodbyes* to American Baptist Pastor and to the little foreign car that served as our latest rescue boat. The pastor informed us that the car wasn't acting right the whole trip down and we prayed over that little car— at least that is what it appeared. In reality, we were praying over this big broken hulk of a man who felt like a helpless little child. We never saw American Baptist Pastor again, nor did we talk to him. But I am certain to this very day he occasionally stops to thank the Maker for his visit with three helpless gypsies and the Methodist preacher's car.

That night, we stayed in the basement of Charles and Martha Bass. Charles was on staff at the little church that hosted the youth event. A summer earlier our friend, Jeromy, from the little apartment, spent a summer there. Four years later, my wife, Julie, would sleep in that house for five weeks while she completed her college coursework with an internship in Colorado Springs.

A year after that, along with Scott and his wife and Jeromy and his wife, we moved to Monument to help a new church get started a few miles down the road. Julie and I lived in that basement for a month. I love it when a family dedicates the use of their stuff to others who are on a journey alongside them.

The Bass' love others on the journey of faith! The Maker says that others will know that we have been revolutionized when people see our love for one another. From the future looking back, it is so clear how this experience was part of the bigger plan. No fiction writer could write that well; I am humbled by the reality of the Maker and His ways.

I will never be the same.

We arose early the next morning to hitch a ride in a hippie van with the hippie youth pastor's wife who served at Monument Hill and hosted our event the night before. The ride back to Limon was routine and anti-climactic and we arrived at the garage to find the ARK02 ready to hit the road again with two new fuel pumps. I looked at the mechanic and asked him how much the repair would cost us. He calmly looked me in the eye and said, "It'll be eight hundred dollars."

The three gypsies turned white as we watched hope drain from the top of our heads to the bottom of our feet, but no one knew what was in the inside pocket of my largest suitcase.

We unpacked all of the gear in the bungee web and pulled my navy blue American Tourister bag from underneath the mess. I reached in and pulled out the last of my student loan money. I had not told either of the other gypsies that I had eight, hundred-dollar bills with me "just in case." So there in Limon, Colorado, I left behind a few things: my pride, my doubt and my eight-hundred-dollar security blanket. With that, I left my last shred of human provision. Off we went, headlong into the danger of His adventure and the safety of His provision.

Every time I think back on these stories, I am astonished how the Maker walks ahead of us as we go. It is true that no fiction author could write a story this clever. Theologians call it "prevenient grace," the grace that walks before us. Other folks call it "luck" or "coincidence." I am not that smart, nor am I that naive. I just call him "Daddy." The Maker gives and the Maker takes away, but the Maker never leaves us stranded alone as we pursue the "what ifs" and "why nots" that He sets before us.

American Baptist Pastor and the Gypsies Praying Over the Rescue Boat

From Colorful to Majestic

"But we all, with unveiled face, beholding as in a mirror the glory of the Lord, are being transformed into the same image from glory to glory, just as from the Lord, the Spirit." *The Compass,* II Corinthians 3:18

We left Colorful Colorado with our next planned stop being the majestic Canadian Rockies and eastern Alaska. In more ways than one, we had no idea what we were headed into. The trip into Wyoming and Montana was uneventful, as most of it was in the darkness of night. We stopped at a little pull-off on the side of the road to sleep in central Wyoming and then arrived early in the morning for a drive through Yellowstone. There is obviously no way to experience the full beauty of that park in a day, but we saw enough to be inspired for the remainder of the journey northward to Calgary and the Canadian Rockies. I remember my perspective of America expanding that day; I never knew how beautiful and expansive this home of mine was. A sojourner can never wrap his or her mind around the variety of people, culture and landscape of America the Beautiful without a trip across the country.

Border Crossing

Late that night after a long day in Yellowstone, we were on our way to the border crossing into Alberta, Canada, via I-15 and Sweet Grass, Montana. We expected the doorway between the U.S. and Canada to simply be like a drive-thru window and a flash of our identification cards. We anticipated we would be on the road again in ten minutes, especially since our rite of passage took place in the middle of the night or early in the morning; I am not sure which. How busy could a border station be at that hour of the day?

We pulled up to the stop gate and Scott stuck his head outside the window for a quick chat with the border officer. In a moment, our short stop at a drive-thru window turned into a two-hour visit with multiple officers in an early morning interrogation of the three gypsies in pursuit of adventure.

"Could you all step out of the car please?"

Awakening from a half-sleep state, I peered through cloudy eyes to see a uniformed officer asking the question that you never want to hear. We all stepped out to questions about weapons and illegal drugs, livestock and invasive pests. (How could we be transporting a head of cattle in a Ford Bronco, anyway?) We complied with every request and answered every ridiculous question. As the officer began to dig into the bungee web, we were asked to unpack our belongings for further investigation of our traveling agenda.

The next step was an individual interrogation to confirm that our stories matched. I cannot remember who was first, but I remember the sweat beginning to pour out of my forehead on that cool morning somewhere between the U.S. and southwest Canada. Not only was the officer asking me scary questions, he even shined a big round light in my eyes, just like in the movies. I tried to squeak honest answers through my quivering lips. I was anxiously hoping that everything I said dovetailed with the other gypsies. We all answered honestly, as ridiculous as our stories sounded. I cannot speak for the other gypsies, but I personally would have questioned my story too if I was the one asking the questions.

Border Patrol: "So, tell me where you live."

Kevin: "Cullman, Alabama...well...actually Florence, Alabama where I go to college."

Border Patrol: "When did you leave Florence, Alabama?"

Kevin: "Three days ago, well, I think it was three, or maybe four, it's been a long trip and the days kinda get mixed up."

Border Patrol: "Where is your final destination?"

Kevin: "Anchorage, Alaska...well, actually it's Wasilla, Alaska I think. We are staying at a youth camp there."

Border Patrol: "Why are you traveling to Wasilla, Alaska?"

Kevin: "Well...the three of us are on a sort of mission trip."

Border Patrol: "What organization are you traveling with?"

Kevin: "Um...well...we are just on our own, we are not traveling with any organization."

Border Patrol: "What are you going to do when you get there?"

Kevin: "We are going to do some stuff around the youth camp where we are staying."

Border Patrol: "Do you know when you plan to arrive?"

Kevin: "Probably sometime tomorrow."

Border Patrol: "How much money are you carrying on you right now?"

Kevin: "I am not really sure, but I think Scott has about three hundred dollars. I spent mine getting our truck repaired in Colorado."

Border Patrol: "Thank you, wait in the lobby please."

A few minutes later, the officer in charge got us back together and smiled as he walked into the room.

"Boys, first I want to say that we really respect what you are doing. We believe your intentions are good. Secondly, I want to say that you have no idea what you are getting yourself into. You left from north Alabama and are headed to Wasilla, Alaska. You will be surprised to know that you are about halfway there."

The three gypsies turned white once again.

"Furthermore, you are heading for the Alaska Highway before tourist season begins and the gas stations are only open from six a.m. to six p.m. and spaced about a hundred miles apart on average. You have little money and a vehicle that is not prepared to make the long journey across the Canadian Rockies and the St. Elias Mountain Range. We cannot force you to return, but we strongly suggest you rethink your trip."

Once again, that familiar foe of fear visited me as we sat in that little interrogation chamber. I teetered once again considering how I could convince Scott that we may have bitten off more than we could chew. But fear could not conquer resolve. Resolve would not bow to reason. Reason could not swallow our passion for adventure. It became clear to me all over again that we were bound for Alaska. John Wayne once said, "Courage is being scared to death...and saddling up anyway."

We had already been through so much together and with the Maker at that point, so we saddled up once again and the ARK02, with the three gypsies, left that border crossing with more resolve than ever as we headed to Dawson Creek, British Columbia, Canada, to hop onto the "World Famous Alaska Highway."

Taming the Stallion Heart

As we drove through southwest Canada with a new resolve, we also began to realize we had a new awareness of what it might look like to follow the Maker into dangerous territory. To this day, I am unsure how we paid for the gas to Anchorage and beyond, but somehow the wheels on our rolling rescue boat continued to turn.

One night before we reached the Alaska Highway, I was driving the ARK02 and stopped for a quick cup of coffee and snack to keep me awake for a few more hours. Once again, it was late and I was tired—Scott was napping in the passenger seat and Keith was dead to the world in the sleep cabin. I chatted with the attendant at the checkout counter and heard the Maker whisper in my ear to share with him the Good News that the Maker has sent Redeemer to make us new. Timidity convinced me to back off. I wandered away and took the lonely path of rebellion. After all, we were running on a tight schedule and we didn't have time to extend our stay at a temporary oasis. Anyway, he probably wouldn't listen and he was probably too tired to comprehend if he did.

Forty-five minutes down the road, I could not help myself: the inner stallion had to be tamed. I woke the guys up and said, "Guys, I am so sorry, but I have to back track about forty miles." I had been driving at a snail's pace the past half hour because I couldn't decide whether to push forward or return to my place of rebellion. Together, the gypsies decided that obedience was our priority and we turned around.

I rehearsed over and over what I would say to the man behind the counter; I knew my lines like a famous actor ready for a day on the set of an A film. I confidently exited the ARK02 and headed for the door of the oasis and walked up to the man behind the counter and declared, "I was in here about an hour and a half ago and I feel like God sent me to tell you He loves you." The reply was both a wrecking ball and a radical relief to me.

"I know that. He lives in my heart. Thanks, man."

An hour and a half of precious time out of the way; a wrestling in my soul about returning or continuing onward; a battle with the stallion on whether it was worth it; a rehearsing of my lines to make sure I was prepared for the moment—it was all summed up with two simple, yet profound, words, "Thanks man."

Did I miss the voice of the Maker? Was it my guilt-laden conscience speaking instead? Had my APPS extended into my relationship with God until it had turned into a mere performance for Him? Was I just losing my freaking mind? Or could this have been a test of obedience?

As I write these words, I still can't sort it out. What I do know is that the wild stallion inside me was both tamed and freed at the same time. For it is in obedience that we find freedom—it is in submitting to a Master that we find our liberty; it is in releasing our control that we are released in our soul.

When I was a youngster, Scott and I loved to ride three-wheelers through the pine forests of north Alabama. We longed to be off-road. We loved to be outside the path laid out for us. We would climb hills and fly through knee-deep mud pits—we would carve our own path. It felt like true freedom.

I remember the day we found "the hill." It was the steepest climb we'd found on the couple-hundred-acre forest we frequented on our three-wheeled crafts that transported us to other worlds. "Man, that would be fun to climb," I thought. Scott was already on his first ascent. I took off behind him. Little did I know, there was a big hole about two-thirds the way up. My wheel fell into that hole and the momentum shifted just enough to send my three-wheeled spacecraft flipping upside down and rolling all the way to the bottom of the hill. I hung on for dear life, like a bull rider in the finals of the big rodeo refusing to let go of the rope. I should've died—I didn't.

A couple of days later we discovered another adventure in the same forest, hidden deep in the recesses of our three-wheeler playground—a race-track! It was created some years earlier for some other space travelers on some other spacecraft. We took our first lap slowly, checking for obstacles and dangers. The turns were carved out perfectly so you could take them at "superblast" speeds and ride the curvature right around into the next straight away. Man, could we fly on that track!

As I reflect on freedom, I realize that there is so much value in running the course set out for you. The adventure is just as exciting, but there is an assurance that someone has gone before and carved out the danger spots and filled in the holes.

He knows the very path that will provide us with all we need to fulfill the adventurous desires of our heart. He knows. Obedience is the path to true freedom— freedom to explore the vast paths set out before you and to still know that the One who holds the blueprints of your soul has gone before you making the paths straight. He is for us and not against us. He is the very One who planted that desire for adventure deep down in our hearts and He longs for us to experience it as it was meant to be.

Forty-five minutes later, with Scott at the wheel, we returned to where my newfound freedom began. Although it felt like I had lost the battle, I knew I had made significant progress toward winning the war against the part of me that wants to do it my way.

A Parking Lot Epiphany

The Alaska Highway is much like the figurative "wormhole" in modern astrological studies and science fiction. A wormhole is a connecting bridge from one region of space time to another; for example, it may be the bridge from galaxy to galaxy. They are theoretical tunnels that allow travel from one universe to another, which would in essence allow one to travel through time. Yep...that is the Alaska Highway. It is the bridge that connects civilization to wilderness, the 21st century to the past and one form of reality to another. For someone or something traversing the "wormhole," the journey can be chaotic and even dangerous at times, particularly back in 1996 before tourist season began.

One dilemma that we faced in the wormhole, which we did not anticipate until our border crossing, was the necessity to wait for resources. The only time I have ever had to wait for fuel was in the line when the two service stations near my home were having a price war. Was there anywhere in the world that you still had to sit and wait for something so available and so necessary? I was naïve, having never traveled to a third world country or remote part of the globe.

It was true. The gas stations were only open from six to six and when you arrived after six in the evening, you waited until morning to fill your tank. We stopped at a little oasis and struck up a conversation with an attendant who was kind enough to supply us with a hand-sketched table showing gas sources and the distance between them along the Alaska Highway. Our first night beyond civilization on the highway was intimidating.

We stopped for gas at a little motel/convenience store as close to 6 p.m. as we could and then drove until we knew that we didn't have the fuel to arrive at the next. We had to stop.

We pulled into the next small parking lot— well, I say parking lot, but in reality it was just a plot of dirt in the middle of a forested area with a tiny building and a single gas pump—it was obvious that the attendant lived at the station, but there was nothing we could do to fill our tank. Our only option was to wait until six the next morning.

We pulled the ARK02 into a grassy area and parked next to an old gas tanker truck with "RESTAURANT" painted in bold letters across the tank that once rescued gypsies like us from the side of the Alaska Highway. Now the truck was just used to catch passersby's attention as they whizzed past the last stop for gas and food for the next hundred miles.

The reality of fatigue settled in on the three gypsies and we realized it was time to get some rest. Much to our surprise, Keith overcame his fear and set up his little temporary bedroom outdoors. Scott tucked in with the shelter of the sleep cabin, and I could not sleep. I took a short walk. This was the first time I had spent any significant amount of time in absolute silence in the wilderness. ABSOLUTE silence. It was deafening.

Our Overnight Wait for Fuel

Occasional bellows from large animals were the only signs of life outside of the gypsies.

In north Alabama, the crickets and frogs provide a symphony of sound after dark, but in the depths of the arctic wilderness, the sound of a cricket would have shattered the silence barrier like a military fighter jet breaking the sound barrier. Yes, it was the combination of total solitude and the faint occasional sounds of distant wildlife that penetrated my heart most deeply that first night in the Canadian Wilderness. I think that was the first time I realized that this experience really would be different from life in rural Alabama.

But the most puzzling difference about this first night in the wilderness was the dusk-like state of the night even at eleven. It was dark, to be sure, but looking westward toward our destination, the sun was barely bedding down in the nest of trees and brush that covered the horizon. It was as if she wanted to peek her head out from under the covers to take a look at what was going on with the gypsies and ARK02...as if we were the imaginary monsters in her closet.

I cannot remember knowing that this would happen. In my ignorance, I didn't anticipate that things would be much different with the way nature works, no matter how far away we traveled. If there is one thing in life I thought you could count on as a constant, it was seasons and days and moon phases and that the sun will set at the end of the day. I couldn't help being curious about that, for I felt sure the world operated just the same no matter where I would find myself.

Peering through the wormhole, I began to wonder more intently what things would be like on the other side. The things I thought I was sure about began to get a little fuzzy. I was entering a new reality and it was a little uncomfortable.

My grandmother Beasley always told me that when I was a baby that I would fight against sleep with everything in me. I still do till this day—as a matter of fact, I am writing this sentence at two in the morning. Sleep finally began to win the battle in the parking lot. As my heavy eyelids closed the chapter on this experience, I curled up in my sleeping bag and let the stallion wander off into another wormhole—the bridge between today and tomorrow.

The next morning, we awoke safe from the bears and moose that Keith was so sure would take our lives at such an early age. The attendant of the oasis was already at his workstation. We fueled up and were off once again for the next mile of the wormhole.

I realized that night in the parking lot that I was not as aware of the world as I would have liked to believe. There have been many times throughout the journey of life that I have sailed across an ocean of ignorance; just to find that what lie on the other side was deeper depths of the same.

In high school, I assumed I had arrived at a place no one else had been and that my purpose in life was to beckon others to come. Since then, I have realized that a much better use of my life is to stop using my mouth and start using my ears, listening for others who have gone before and following those small voices to new places and new understanding. When I seem to be losing my way I listen again—intent on discerning the voices and consciously choosing which to follow, all the while listening for the smallest, yet most life-giving voice of all...the voice of the Spirit of the Maker.

Life itself is a wormhole of sorts—a pathway leading from one reality to another. The journey in between can lead to lots of bumps and bruises; it can disorient and confuse, but when we exit on the other side, the destination will be more than we can imagine and will make the journey worth it.

Keith after the Longest Night of His Life

The Light at the End of the Tunnel

"Cool! Look at that little mountain ahead of us."

I had completed my tour in the sleep cabin and had grabbed the wheel again to take us a few more miles through the wormhole. It was the first small mountain we had seen in a good while. Although the Canadian Rockies provided some wonderful opportunities to spot wildlife and enjoy mountain scenery, we were tired of the small mountains and anxious to see the "Big Ones" as we came closer to our destination.

Maybe this would be the beginning of the Alaskan experience, I thought as I drove.

The little mountain ahead of us seemed to grow by the foot every few miles. Slowly, I began to realize that this was not a little mountain a few miles away, but that it was a monster of a mountain many miles away. I remember the next hour or so as a period of anticipation and excitement to see what lay ahead. The little molehill continued to grow just like those little dinosaurs my kids put in a bowl of water overnight that expand to fourteen times their size. When we were close enough to take in its magnitude, we were not disappointed—it was magnificent! The first sight of the St. Elias Mountain Range and Kluane Lake was breathtaking! It looked as if we were going to drive right into the side of the mountain. As we were getting closer and closer, I began to wonder if the mountain would open up and swallow us whole.

A stop sign began to take shape ahead of us: *A stop sign?* We had not seen one of those in what seemed like days. On a journey that launches someone into a new way of life, something as simple as a stop sign can take on a whole meaning of its own. What seemed so commonplace in our comfort zone can feel so out of place when we are far from home.

What was once the support structures that kept us from crashing became the wrecking ball that sent it back into its broken places. The thing that seemed so familiar became a stranger in our newfound land. A right turn led us into a journey that would last for quite some time as for miles we were hugged tightly by two new friends: the St. Elias' on one side and the Kluane Lake on the other, and there was barely enough room in between to breathe. It was clear that I had known God, but for the first time I realized that I had not known a Maker who was big enough to do that!

My life drastically changed during this leg of the journey because for the first time in my life I fell in love with the Maker's work. And as I did so, I fell more in love with the Maker Himself. A new sense of purity in our relationship rose slowly like the feeling you get on a cool March morning in north Alabama when you see the first signs of spring begin to appear. Life began to look different that day; I sensed that things were changing in me that would last for the rest of my life. Nothing was the same from that point on.

This was the first of many times in Alaska that I realized things are not always as they appear. And the larger the context, the more confusing the perspective can be. What looks to be an hour's easy hike turns into a six-hour journey through hell. What appears to be a small hill to breeze over, turns into a full-scale mountain that has to be climbed. It is much the same in life. Those things that we fear the most, often offer the least danger. It is the little things that can kill us. Integrity when no one is looking; little white lies that seem to do no harm; just a few minutes with a friend who leads us down the wrong path…those are the mountains on the horizon that grow larger as we journey.

I also learned how to anticipate great things. We see only a glimpse of our future with the Maker. Anytime we stand beside a vast ocean and watch the waves crash against the white sand; when we peer off the side of a cliff to see farther than we have seen before and notice that our life is not as large as we once thought; when a father sits at his wife's side in a delivery room and watches his new baby girl take her first gasp of air, something changes. We see into an unexplainable world where this life meets the next, we sense the Maker closer to us than we ever thought He could be, and our sense of curiosity and wonder about life with Him is made more alive. It is no wonder that folks such as Corrie Ten Boom and Mother Theresa, who have seen more than we will ever see, have such an acute desire to "go home" to their Maker—they see home so much more clearly.

When I was a teenager I came to know God. The little faith community that I attended used the King James Version of the Bible. I remember pondering a verse and wondering what it meant: It read, "But we all, with open face beholding as in a glass the glory of the Lord, are changed into the same image from glory to glory, even as by the Spirit of the Lord." That was a lot to take in for a youngster who had no experience with the Bible. As I think back upon this story, it all comes together like the last piece of puzzle to complete a tiny section of that five thousand-piece jigsaw on my grandma's coffee table. When things seem too big, you celebrate the small victories…the completion of a small section knowing that the entire puzzle is too much to hope for.

We travel from peak to peak on the journey of life. We can't take in the whole picture, so the Maker gives it to us in pieces. We'll be minding our business one day, taking care of the daily grind, and it will hit us; the final piece to complete one little chunk of glory in this faith journey. Like the proverbial light bulb going off, it hits us on our blind side. In a moment we have a clearer revelation because a piece of the puzzle just fell into place. We moved from a past reality into a present newness; we've passed through another wormhole; we see the Maker just a bit more clearly; we understand our wife just a little bit more deeply; we grasp our unreasonable response to pain with a little more insight; we move from Glory to Glory; we blink our eyes and are conformed into a more clear reflection of the Redeemer. This is the journey from Colorful to Majestic.

That is the life of adventure. We travel beyond the "what ifs" and the "why nots" and all of the sudden we see a God big enough to carve out those mountains one cut at a time. And we marvel!

The Pivot Point

"We are made in the image of God; we carry within us the desire for our true life of intimacy and adventure. To say we want less than that is to lie." - John Eldredge, The Journey of Desire: Searching for the Life We Always Dreamed of[5]

From Whitehorse to Haines Junction and onward beyond the Canada/Alaska border we made it to our destination state of Alaska! The gypsies were exhausted and in a daze, and the ARK02 was holding on for dear life, but we made it. I can't remember what we were eating or how often we were stopping, but it was minimal at best. A western turn at Glenallen near the Wrangell-St. Elias Mountains propelled us toward the last leg of our long journey. Finally, we arrived in Wasilla and meandered around until we found our way to the Laverne Griffin Baptist Youth Camp, our home away from home for the next few days and the place the gypsies would leave as different people.

When I was in high school marching band, we would spend hours practicing precision turns. Each foot would drop down right on top of where the foot of the last marcher departed and I would spin my weight around quickly to make a swift and precise turn toward my new direction. The turf under that spot was worn down to the red clay of north Alabama; little did I know this small youth camp in south-central Alaska would be a similar pivot point for the rest of my life. Just a few days there would launch me into a new destiny and would impact the rest of my college career, my partner for life, my first two years of marriage and just about everything that would follow.

Pivot points usually show up in unexpected places. They are often the result of heartache and sometimes even tragedy, while other times they come as silent as the morning sun peeking her head slowly over the eastern horizon. When they come through life events we often feel torn, like that turf underneath the marcher's foot. In a moment, life can take on a totally new meaning and the trajectory of our existence is redirected. I have come to embrace those times. They are the most difficult days on our journey, but they can be the most significant. During the short redirects that come from time to time, the majority of our major life decisions are made.

Imagine the young man who has been frustrated about finding his future mate. He has given up and resigned to bachelorhood. Then along comes the girl who captures his heart, and within a week he has landed in the trappings of love. Trajectory changes.

Then there's the young lady who has an unquenchable longing to hold her baby. She and her husband sit in the doctor's office as the news puts a death grip on the depths of her soul. "We can consider some alternatives, but there's a one percent chance that your body can conceive a child." She is left to sort out what it means and pray for a miracle.

Emotions rage. Dreams are born or die. The turf tears and soon begins to grow again. These pivot points, in one way or another, are the beginning of the end of one way of life and give birth to another. One that seems less secure...vulnerable.

Andy Gullahorn said it well in these lyrics, "You have to tear it apart to get the pieces to mend. Strange place to start—beginning of the end." It has been said that we often have to go backward to move forward. It is true. As much as it hurts, tearing up what has been built can be the first step to rebuilding what was meant to be in the first place.

Our Newfound Family

When we rounded the last turn in the long dirt driveway entering the pivot point, we saw the patriarch of our new family coming out to meet us. He was not a notable figure from his appearance—he was medium sized, medium build and bald on top. Larry greeted us kindly, but without much emotion. We were as much a mystery to him as he was to us, but little did we know he and his family would become a gift from the Maker in the coming days. He showed us to our quarters: just a humble cabin we would share as a team in the days to come. The bathhouse was some distance away and the kitchen and chapel was a short hike down the hill. The gypsies were ecstatic and a five-star all-inclusive resort would not have made us more content!

Our first order of business was to pop loose the straps of the bungee web and unload some of our stuff. We left Larry and looked back at the ARK02—she was a disaster, caked with mud, glacier silt and who knows what else. She was hardly recognizable as a rescue boat. She had all the markings of a warhorse back from taking her knight in shining armor into a fierce battle. Somewhere along the way, one of the gypsies had scribbled with his finger through the dirt on the back windshield, "Alaska or Bust" and it was barely visible underneath the miles worth of dust that had settled on top.

After unpacking a few of our belongings, we headed straight for the showers. We had not had the luxury for a few days and there was an indistinguishable odor among the gypsies and the sleeping quarters. It was an odd smell that I can't even begin to explain. That will be left to your imagination.

After showers, we had a visit with Sharon, Larry's wife; Brad, thirteen and Ashley, twelve. Some people you know for years and it seems they are still strangers, others you know for a day and no number of years could bring you closer. Often, these types of experiences happen at those pivot points in your life; times when you have turned away from the things of the past and gone headlong into the things of the future; when your soul is vulnerable. The Hales were the latter. They had moved to Alaska a couple years before as a missionary family. We would hear so many stories during our short stay with them; the Maker had most definitely planned their move to Alaska and they were happy to oblige, even through the tough climate and difficult challenges of life on a small summer camp in the middle of Alaska.

In a recent conversation, Sharon told me a story of their first year in Alaska. The water pipes in their small mobile home were rusted when they first arrived. In the wintertime they would have to run to the bathhouse some distance away, take showers and run back "home" with towels wrapping their heads. She said that when they arrived back to the safety of their trailer, the towels would be frozen like stone. Like hurdles in a sprinter's race, they leapt over the struggles, one by one, in hot pursuit of the call the Maker had shouted at them, "Go to Alaska and meet me there! You will get further instructions when you need them. No matter what you do, just don't turn back!"

I cannot describe the joy in the heart of the gypsies that day. We had set out on our own pursuit of the voice of the Maker and we had arrived. The journey through the wormhole brought with it a freedom that could not have come through any other source. Had the Maker shouted any other directive, the journey wouldn't have brought such joy—it came through believing and stepping out into the unknown. It required a step of blind faith.

Whether the exhilaration was the relief of arriving alive, or the excitement of realizing the impossible had happened, we didn't know, and we didn't care. All we knew was that we were different people from when we departed a week ago. We had seen the hand of God at work protecting, guiding and providing for us. How could one live that much life in such a short time?

How we experience time has always puzzled me. There are experiences when a moment seems like a day and others when a day seems like a moment. I occasionally ponder the Maker's ability to live outside the limits of His creation. With a few brush strokes any artist can change the reality of a story he has painted. An artist has the ability to transcend the reality of the world he has put on canvas and he has the right to change it. Maybe that's how the Maker can reside anywhere at any time in the history of His masterpiece and not be any less present at any other place or time in the same. Maybe that's how He can be ever changing and always the same. Maybe that's how He can know all things and still give us an option to choose our own path. I wonder if it's a possibility that when we die we are immediately taken up to Him and at the same time we rise up in the air with Him when Redeemer returns for his children?

When we are experiencing bliss it seems that "time flies." Could it be that in those moments we are caught up into another world where the measure of time changes...or doesn't exist at all? Could it be a sneak peek into eternity? Maybe time is a necessary part of the fallen nature of man that we have created to simply measure the length of days and the years of life in a primitive attempt to control it. Or maybe the Maker created time to mark our days and allow us the opportunity of measuring our experience here so we can look forward to what lies beyond this leg of the journey.

One day we will know.

The Maker gave us the gift of each other that week. It was found wrapped up around a campfire, at the beach as we sifted sand removing small rocks so children could laugh and play, fishing at midnight in the twilight and roasting our catch on the open fire as we sang and laughed. He has a knack for picking out just the perfect gift. It may not be extravagant and it may not be the one everyone else is looking for, but it is perfectly fitted for each of us. And for that I am thankful!

Our stay was filled with projects around the camp. We sifted sand, cleaned boats, cut grass on the ball field and cleaned cabins.

We spent a night with a youth group at Big Lake Baptist Church and spoke to the kids of the Bible study group on the camp, but, other than that, our time was spent with each other. The Maker spoke to our hearts both individually and through each other in that little short-term community we formed on the shore of Kalmbach Lake.

Our Home Away From Home

A Few Days Later...

There is a book worth of stories that took place in the few days at the pivot point, some of which I will share in the following pages; others will go untold until we are sitting around the campfire after we pass through the wormhole of life. What matters most is that none of them would have taken place had the Maker not weaved the gypsies' hearts together with the pure and unblemished hearts of our new "family!" There are some things in life we can do alone, but the greatest of experiences happen with others along the journey. That is the essence of community, especially community among followers of Redeemer.

Dancing on the Glacier

"So if the Son sets you free, you will be free indeed. - *The Compass,* John 8:36

Who could possibly drive forty-eight hundred miles over the course of a week to one of the most beautiful places on the planet and not spend at least a day seeing the things that cannot be seen back home? We had too much invested to miss out on the sights, sounds, culture, wildlife and wilderness of Alaska.

The three gypsies and a thirteen-year-old stowaway, named Brad Hale, loaded up the rescue boat, ARK02, and headed southeast beyond Anchorage along Seward Highway and the Turnagain Arm to see the famous Portage Glacier.

In 1996, the glacier was still visible and accessible from the parking lot of the current visitor center, which was built in 2001. It has since receded and left only fragments of the original glacier and a lake to house its remnant melt and silt left behind by its slow death.

The drive was breathtaking: the glacier no less so. When we left Wasilla the weather was perfect for an outing. By the time we made the hundred-mile trip to the frozen lake cutting through the Portage Valley, the unpredictable Alaskan weather had turned into a freezing mix of rain and strong winds. To this day, I cannot sort out what happened in our hearts as we drove the road leading to the mouth of the glacier. That cold rain washed away the fallow top layer of dirt on our hearts. That strong wind blew all the remnants of garbage that was left in our minds. When we arrived at the mouth of the glacier, not a word was spoken. We were probably frozen for a moment in absolute awe. One of the gypsies swung open the door of ARK02 and we were off. We ran, jumped, danced and screamed at the top of our lungs like little schoolboys after winning the county tee-ball championship.

It was a community experience for sure, but only following the emancipation of our souls from the brokenness and bondage that the life of a typical late teenager has pent up in his cage of fear, insecurity and anxiety about the future. From the time a boy is able to comprehend life he is asking one question, "Do I have what it takes?"

The climax of the wrestling match, with that question, often occurs in the late teenage years into the early twenties. If a boy is not able to resolve an answer to that question, it can be tragic. "Do I have what it takes to be a man?" "Do I have what it takes to please a woman?" "Do I have what it takes to be all the Maker created me to be?"

That question was answered for me that day as we danced on a glacier. I'm not sure what happened with the other gypsies, but God dropped that answer right into the crevices of my heart where it would find a home forever.

"Yes. You have exactly what you need to be all that I've created you to be."

Confidence and security comes when we see ourselves as God sees us. Through the course of life, our enemy has whispered thousands of sweet nothings into our unshielded ears, luring us to believe his lie. He tells us over and over that we are not good enough, strong enough, smart enough or brave enough.

The truth is, apart from the empowering of the Spirit of the Maker, we are none of those, but as we invite Him into our lives, we have every resource we need to be, do and act as the Masterpiece He created us to be (Ephesians 2:10). When we allow ourselves to be immersed in the Holy Spirit, everything changes.

That was something to celebrate!

I'm not sure how long this party lasted, but it was too long to be running around in freezing rain and wind. The warmth in our hearts surely must have kept us from a mild case of hypothermia.

After our individual celebrations of liberty, we huddled together for hugs and congratulations from one another. Then we hopped right back into the ARK02 and headed into town for a little visit to civilization. Anchorage has most of the comforts of home and lots of things to do for the visitor from a faraway land. The gypsies welcomed a short visit back to normal...well, relative normal.

Not Just Any Old Pair of Shoes

Brad loved shoes!

I have never seen anything like it before or since. He was a young boy who had an overwhelming attachment to sneakers. He would work for his parents, save his allowance, pinch his pennies and whatever else he had to do to drive to Anchorage and pick up his next pair. He had his eye on a pair of red Air Jordans, size eleven and a half.

It was a special day when the family would hop in the car and make the drive to Anchorage. Brad would protect the dollars in his pocket with security measures no less secure than Fort Knox. Those dollars were precious to him, not because they had inherent value themselves, but because they represented his next adventure with his new Nikes or Reeboks or whatever the latest fad required. He had been saving up for some time when the gypsies arrived at the pivot point. Brad had the feeling like a mother would have had eight and a half months into a pregnancy. "I wish this baby would just hurry up and come out, I am tired of waiting. This is hard work."

Something unexpected happened to Brad at the arrival of the gypsies. Brad fell in love. Not a romantic love, but the kind of love a soldier has with a fellow warrior in the trenches. A love that has no bounds and is not based on what one offers another, but just rises right up out of the depths of who we are in our heart. I'm sure Brad must have been lonely. He was all by himself in a big world of insecurity and boredom (at least for a thirteen-year-old) that life on a summer camp at the end of a long winter could offer. He needed companionship and he needed to feel like he was not alone. Keith offered that to him more than the other gypsies.

Apart from the Maker, Brad was the main character in Keith's Alaska story and Keith in Brad's. That is why Brad, the stowaway, traveled southeast with us that cold rainy day in June.

After dancing on the glacier, we made our obligatory souvenir shop stops in downtown Anchorage. Who would travel to a place so far away without a drink at the fountain of the local market? These souvenirs are the same in almost every city around the world. Depending on the level of civilization, they may differ in quality and source. The third world countries offer higher quality hand-made items while the first world countries carry cheap assembly line look-alikes. But the variety and types bear no striking differences.

We shopped from aisles of statues of local animals, T-shirts and sweatshirts that decked the halls, rocks carved into various local shapes and figures, ball caps, cigarette lighters, candy, stuffed animals, etc. Small symbols of a traveler's experiences made to be purchased and then taken home and placed on a shelf to serve as small windows through which the traveler can return to a time when the worries of life were put on temporary hold in order to experience a glimpse of eternity. Isn't that what vacation is anyway; an opportunity to experience the life we long for, which in reality, can only be found on the other side of life?

Much like the wardrobe in C.S. Lewis' Chronicles of Narnia, we step through and get a glimpse of what life is really all about and then we return without a minute lost to the world that has been corrupted by things that really don't even matter. Those impostors seem to pull the curtains to what is really going on behind the scenes, a beautiful story of the redemption of Creation.

I always thought it unusual when we hit the pause button of life and journey to an unknown land. A fresh perspective usually accompanies us as we travel. A week or a month later, the time doesn't really matter; we return to the "reality" that we left. Nothing has changed. In fact, it almost seems that time stopped when we left, or even worse, went backwards and left us behind on schedules and deadlines. It's almost as if I can feel the wild and free self that I find on the journey being sucked right out by the reality that I find when I return. The truth is that the reality is in the freedom we find when peering through the window of what will be on the other side of the wormhole of life.

Maybe that's what the gypsies were looking for in this journey. Maybe that is what the Maker had in mind when He whispered in Scott's ear in that little college town apartment a few months before. Maybe He wanted to let us peer for a moment through the window in order to have a clearer view of Him. Maybe He wanted us to start our adult lives through the filter of reality…the Maker's reality. A reality that sometimes gets drowned out in the day-to-day grind of 21st century America.

And then Keith spotted it! Keith is a dramatic fella; he is easily excited by the little things in life, like the four-year-old boy in a candy shop. In this little marketplace store in the middle of a crowded city, the world stopped turning and the room lit with rays of light. It didn't seem like a treasure to me, but to Keith it was gold—a print of an eagle in flight mounted on a wooden plaque. Keith had less money than Scott or I and it was not enough for a print of an eagle in flight mounted on a wooden plaque in an overpriced souvenir shop.

I was proud of Keith when he turned his back and walked away from his newest "love at first sight." Then something miraculous happened. As Keith walked out of the overpriced souvenir shop, Brad, the stowaway, pulled his shoe money out of his *Fort Knox* wallet, picked up the print of an eagle in flight mounted on the wooden plaque in the overpriced souvenir shop, walked confidently up to the attendant and threw his *Fort Knox* shoe money on the counter.

For Keith it was a short-lived dream come true, and for the stowaway it was a small step for mankind and a giant leap toward manhood. For when we become men, our decisions to fulfill our own desires or to fulfill another's desires have to be weighed carefully in light of long-term return. The stowaway chose well.

One simple action by one young boy made a radical impact on a fellow journeyman. It is amazing how the little things matter: how one simple act of kindness can radically impact another. Wouldn't it be fun to watch life unfold if we looked for simple opportunities like this every day of our lives? It's just a small inconvenience for us that could make all the difference for those around us. They are simple steps through the doorways of "what ifs" and "why nots."

When we arrived back at the pivot point, Keith ran to Sharon and Larry to show them his new treasure and tell them about the stowaway's leap toward manhood. Those parents were glowing with pride—it must have felt just like when a mother bird sees her chick spread his wings for the first time and launch into an unstable and amateur pattern of flight which will, with practice, lead to the independence of the little guy. How must she feel months later as she watches her little one soar over the Maker's handiwork with a perspective he could not have seen from the ground?

Sometimes we forget that the little ones in our life are destined for adulthood. How we invest in them in the early days will determine the decisions they make later that will change the course of the lives of the people they encounter. What a responsibility and privilege!

It was a beautiful story to watch, but the rest of the story is almost unbelievable.

When the gypsies arrived back to north Alabama, Keith was asked to speak at the Sunday morning gathering of his faith community. He shared of the journey of the gypsies and the passage through the wormhole and the Ark of the Pavement and all the other great stories the gypsies had experienced. Afterwards, a local businessman approached Keith and said, "Keith, I don't know if this will help you out or not, but this week

I was behind my office building and I looked over toward the dumpster and saw a pair of tennis shoes in a box. I went over to take a better look and it was a brand new pair of red shoes. Maybe Brad will like these."

Keith opened the box and found a pair of red Air Jordans, size eleven and a half.

The foe of reason inside me fights against believing that something as trivial as a pair of shoes matters to God. He longs, for some reason, to believe it was just another coincidence. I am not quite sure why he would hope that it was by chance as opposed to by design. I think he feels like it would make the struggle with faith easier. You see, reason loves for things to make sense. He loves to solve problems and check them off as explainable. If they can be solved, then they can be explained. If they can be explained, they can be systemized, predicted, planned for, and controlled. As wild and free as he can be at times, he still loves to maintain control.

The Spirit in me, on the other hand, loves these stories! It energizes him and that feels good. There is no need to explain…just accept.

Those dueling voices in my head often engage in long conversations about stories such as this. Sometimes reason wins out and the conclusion is that it is too good to be true. Other times spirit wins and the conclusion is that some things are just too good to be figured out. The beauty of the relationship between them is that they are both right. It is the Maker's job to sort out the details…it is our job to enjoy the journey.

The Journey Home

"We have all known the long loneliness and we have learned that the only solution is love and that love comes with community."
- Dorothy Day[6]

"The world is so empty if one thinks only of mountains, rivers & cities; but to know someone who thinks & feels with us, & who, though distant, is close to us in spirit, this makes the earth for us an inhabited garden." - Johann Wolfgang von Goethe

Stories Give Us Hope

What became clear to our new family in the days at the camp was that the gypsies were not prepared or resourced to make the long trip home. It was obvious to both the gypsies and the Hales that we had bitten off more than we could chew. How were we to make it home on what we had? What if ARK02 got sick again? What would we eat? Those were questions yet to be answered.

A couple of nights before we left, we were sitting around the Hale's living room enjoying our new family. There must have been a conversation about our trip home. This flipped a switch that opened the floodgate of stories of the Maker's provision in the lives of this family who had given their life to Him.

I will never forget my favorite story that night with the new family. It was a cold winter Sunday morning at the pivot point. There was snow on the ground and the new family was determined to go visit with their faith family on their weekly trek to the family reunion. They had ten dollars left in Larry's pocket, no more and no less. Larry was sure he had heard the Maker whisper in his ear to place half of that money in the collection plate at the family reunion. The other half went to gas in their "rescue boat" that transported them that harsh winter morning. They heard another voice trying to drown out the voice of the Maker, it was not a faint whisper. It must have been the voice of the Antagonist, shouting that the pantry was empty and they had children for whom they were responsible to feed. They chose to tune their ears to the whisperer and spoke back to that still small voice asking Him to provide for their needs as they returned to Him the last of the gift that He had given them. Larry released his grip on the gift as it dropped into the collection plate that morning.

When they returned home there was a message on their answering machine from Jonesboro, Arkansas. Turns out that a friend had been visiting with a group of men. The Hales' name came up and as the group talked with the Maker, He tapped one on the shoulder and said, "The Hales have a financial need, and you need to help?" The men collected money and wired it to the Hales and it would be available within twenty-four hours. They had not told anyone about their situation, nor had anyone hinted that they would help. It was a simple return on an investment. It was the way the Maker worked!

That little story lifted the spirits of the gypsies and they were certain once again that they would arrive safely to north Alabama approximately three weeks from their departure. It would not be easy, nor would it be safe. However, the Maker never points where He doesn't provide. He never has. Why would He start today?

I've shared that little truth many times with my wife in the past decade or so. It is true that He's never left us with a need greater than His provision, although sometimes the landscape looked bleak. What would compel Him to stop providing for our needs today? Nothing. We are His children and He distributes His resources efficiently and strategically to both take care of us and stretch us beyond what we think we can handle. That's how a father trains a child.

Closing a Chapter

Our work was done at the pivot point.

Realizing that we were depending on blind faith to make it home, the Hales passed on a couple hundred dollars and a cooler full of road kill for us to cook on the road. Road kill is universal—the only difference is that the road kill in Alaska is very large! Police departments have sign up lists for non-profit organizations that can use the moose and caribou meat. Laverne Griffin Youth Camp was on that list, thanks to the Maker. The chest freezer in the kitchen was full of road kill and a portion of it would supply us for half our trip home.

We said our goodbyes, snapped a few pictures and loaded up our belongings into the bungee web. We rolled out of the pivot point very different from how we arrived just a few days earlier—with a new perspective of life, God and ourselves that was more exciting, dangerous and alive than we had before. That was the end of our first introduction to this special family.

I spent one month with the Hales a few years later, other than that we rarely see them. Life has a way of diverting our paths toward other pilgrims in other lands. In some ways that is tragic, in others it's beautiful. Some day on the other side of the wormhole called life, or maybe even sooner, we will visit again. We will remember. We will laugh and we will cry. We will return to the purity of a relationship that transcended time and space. We will commune once again.

Over the years I have had to learn to let go of my tight hold on people I am closest to. Whether by death or by some other departure, the paths will diverge. I have decided that even though the body moves on, some things will be left behind. If the relationship was one sent by the Maker, what is left behind will never die. My life will never be the same as it would have been had each person in it not played a part. When we reach the other side of eternity, the Body of Christ, all of it, will be united to share in the Maker forever. That will be quite the family reunion.

Before we made it out of Wasilla, we lost a tire to the elements, so our first couple of hours were spent at a tire garage patching up ARK02. How thankful we were that the Maker allowed this to happen near places that could repair a tire. I am amazed how the little things mean so much when in pursuit of His leading. Little did we know that this was only a pre-cursor for what would come...

The Three Gypsies on our Last Day at the Pivot Point

A Lesson on Community

A day or so into our trip home, Scott and I were sitting in the front of the ARK02. I could not stop talking about this thing or that, which is not uncommon for me. Scott was quietly focused on the road ahead us. He looked over and patiently asked me to stop talking and I returned with a, "fine then"...and kept talking. This interaction led to a somewhat heated discussion and a wonderful display of the selfishness of two best friends, who each had needs, stuck in a truck together with nowhere to run.

I felt offended and I could tell Scott did too.

A few years later, in my first few years of marriage, I was sitting in another rescue boat riding around central Florida with the woman I love deeply. I had laryngitis and my usually quiet, introverted wife needed to talk for some odd reason. We had a similar altercation, but that time around I knew how to handle it just a little bit better. I had said for some years that, until I met Julie, I learned more about marriage from Scott than I had anyone else. Now, obviously, that has changed after thirteen mostly happy years of marriage, but that couple of weeks enduring and enjoying a shared life with two friends was invaluable to learning how to live in true community. For it is in true community that you work through differences and love each other all the more.

Both of these experiences were lessons in learning to live 24/7 with someone you love deeply, even when your differences create tension. There are things that make us friends and there are things that have the potential to make us enemies if we don't choose to connect through a deeper purpose. This is the lesson I learned: it is shared purpose that creates community. Everyone has differences; it's part of what makes us unique. But when we connect with one another for the cause of a greater purpose, we can figure out how to overcome our differences, love one another and work for that purpose.

There's a story in *The Compass* that records a prayer that the Redeemer was praying to the Maker. It's in the book of John, Chapter 17 and it is a beautiful picture of true community. Redeemer prays for Himself and for the people that were closest to Him. Then in the third section of that prayer He prays for those who would, at some time in the future, believe in Him. In other words, He prayed for me, and you too if you have invited Him to journey with you through life. His words were not what I would expect to hear in His prayer for me. There are so many things He could have asked the Maker, but He asked that I would be one with everyone else who believes in Him. And He asked that I would be one with Him just as He is one with his Father. I can't even imagine that kind of unity. Especially in a spiritual culture where there is a multitude of division among His people. That I would be one with them just as Redeemer is one with the Maker...imagine that.

How could it be that I could find unity with people who believe so differently than me on some of the peripheral issues in *The Compass*? How could I share life with folks who worship differently, who have differing political views, who practice their faith differently? What does unity look like when so many things divide us? What would it look like in my town, or the place where you live if God's people chose to put aside differences and unify in a common purpose to see the Maker have His way with us? What aspects of our faith would be the connecting points for our new found unity? What differences are important enough to divide?

What would it take for two people on different faith planes to look at each other and say, "Can you just stop talking for a few minutes? Can we just have a little peace and enjoy the scenery?" Could we put aside the offense and continue driving knowing that underneath those differences that divide there is a greater purpose?

The Redeemer dreamed about a unity like that in his people. I am grateful that He put people in my life who understand it. I am also grateful that He has allowed me to understand it. The challenge now is to live in that understanding; to really put differences aside and find a way to walk in unity with my little corner of the Body of Christ.

Keith and the ARK02 After a Long Trip Home

Breakdown in Regina

Interestingly, I cannot remember much about our trip back across the Alaska border and on through western Canada. I do remember our first stop overnight at a campground on the side of the Alaska Highway. Moose droppings were everywhere and I was a little nervous. We were excited about this respite and set our tent up with laughter in our talks and joy in our hearts. We were glad to be off the road for a bit. We fired up the pit and roasted our road kill and feasted on friendship and good wild game.

Then it started to rain.

There was a pavilion in the camp, so we took our tent down, packed up our gear and threw it in the truck. Our sleeping bags found a home on top of the picnic tables under the pavilion and there we half slept as water droplets fell around us, occasionally targeting our heads and faces. It's amazing how long a night can last when sleep evades and scary sounds invade. We awoke the next morning and headed farther down the road.

I remember a couple of fun stops at a hot springs and the sign farm at Watson Lake. Folks who travel the Alaska Highway stop at Watson Lake and leave a favorite sign brought from home, marking their presence much like the neighbor's black lab would leave on your doorstep. Isn't it funny how timeless those little "Johnny Wuz Here" signatures seem? It also eases the nerves a bit and makes you feel not so far away when you see a sign that once marked the city limits of your hometown. It's just plain fun. Some of those signs are hand-made by the travelers and some are acquired through other means (which we will not speak of here). There are hundreds of them, probably even thousands. It is a sight to behold.

The only other memory I have was of our first paid shower experience. Two dollars and a trip behind the little make-shift service station got you a plywood shower stall and some running water over your head. It was exhilarating considering we had not showered in a couple of days. It was also a little unnerving how it felt like a scene from a cheap horror flick.

Other than that, I must have slept the rest of the traverse of the Alaska Highway.

Somewhere in Regina, Saskatchewan, the ARK02 had to stop again. I can't remember what was ailing her, but I do remember that it took a full day for the part to be acquired from the closest real city.

When we arrived at the garage and realized we were stuck overnight, we asked the mechanic if there was anywhere we could walk to take a shower. He was a large gruff guy, what you would expect from a mechanic in the middle of *nowhereville*, Saskatchewan, Canada, and he reminded me eerily of American Baptist Pastor. They looked a lot alike and intimidated me just the same. "Hell," he said, "don't walk over there, drive my damned old pickup truck."

I've been to a lot of places and it always amuses me when someone talks about all the country hicks in my home state of Alabama. It seems that everywhere I go there is a fair share of the quintessential back-road redneck. Like every other people group, they are the same wherever you find them. The lingo and accent may differ, but the culture is just the same. And I love them. If I had to choose who I wanted to be stranded with in a strange place, I'd pick a redneck any day of the week. They never tire of helping a stranded gypsy. They seem to find their identity in rescuing those stuck in the misfortunes of the daily grind. We need those guys.

We were hesitant about jumping into a total stranger's truck to drive four or five miles to a campground to take a shower and get some rest, but he insisted, so off we went.

Scott jumped into the driver's seat and turned the key. The gears grinded as he slammed the old-school clutch into gear. Keith took the passenger side and I saddled up in the middle. The problem with that, which I did not anticipate when I volunteered to sit in the middle, was the air freshener hanging from the rear view mirror. I bumped my head on it as slowly the fog of the situation cleared and I realized it was shaped like a human figure. A second look and I was eye to eye with a cutout of a nude lady hanging right there from a string for all to see, but mostly me since I was sitting in the middle. It was an awkward scenario indeed. I could not look anywhere, without her kicking me in the nose and reminding me of her looming presence.

It was an awkward scene: three short-term young male missionaries driving a thirty-five year-old borrowed clunker of a pick-up truck to find a shower with a naked woman stuck right in front of our faces. As earlier mentioned, only the Maker can write a story such as this. And so He did.

With the ARK02 patched up once again, we traveled day and night to arrive back at our original starting point at the same little college town apartment we left a couple weeks earlier at the beckoning whisper of the Maker Himself. We clocked 9,774 miles on this journey and it was the beginning of a lifetime of stories from the Alaskan wilderness.

How do you describe the relationship developed between the three gypsies? Well, you just don't. Forty years down the road, or maybe sooner, who knows, we will gather alongside a casket adorned with fresh flowers to say goodbye to one of the three and the remaining two will look each other in the eye and without a word spoken, mutually thank the Maker for a lifetime of stories lived out over the course of a few short days. No one else in the room, or in the world for that matter, would ever be able to understand the silent language we speak, for it is a language birthed only through a shared experience that created its own vocabulary. No more important or less important than the thousands of languages spoken by other pilgrims on other journeys: some were fought on a battlefield while others played on a football field; some experienced beside a hospital bed while others surfaced beside a death bed; some were birthed in a church building while others were discovered in a prison cell. The time, place, or experience is not what sets these gypsies apart as a band—it is the temporary escape from perceived reality and our sense of "togetherness" through the process. It was laced with danger and seasoned with love; it would not have produced the same fruit without either of those.

If you have not had the opportunity to glimpse into our future life with the Maker, you soon will, for it is the grace of God that slides open the shutter to give us a view of the garden in order that our hearts will long for Him and our mind will not be stilled until we pass over into the other side of the wormhole to see Him as He is and each other as we were always meant to be.

Celebrating another Victory

Adventures with New Best Friends

"Friendship is born at that moment when one person says to another: What! You too? I thought I was the only one" - C.S. Lewis[7]

"My story is important not because it is mine, God knows, but because if I tell it anything like right, the chances are you will recognize that in many ways it is also yours...it is precisely through these stories in all their particularity, as I have long believed and often said, that God makes Himself known to each of us more powerfully and personally. If this is true, it means that to lose track of our stories is to be profoundly impoverished not only humanly but also spiritually."
- Frederick Buechner

A year passed without much consideration of Alaska, other than the amazing stories we were able to share with family and friends.

We had all but lost touch with the crew at the pivot point. Keith had wandered off to a new life without the other two gypsies. I took off for Lakeland, Florida, in pursuit of the whisper in my ear one of those silent nights in the college apartment when the voice of God spoke during our fifteen-day spiritual focus. Scott stayed behind at the University of North Alabama for a semester before joining me in another adventure at

Southeastern Bible College. We often told stories and reminisced about our journey in 1996.

While attending classes at Southeastern University, we met Elisabeth Griesmer. Elisabeth was born and raised in Wasilla and we got to know her well. It's funny how connecting with her somehow kept us connected with the experience of '96. Kindred spirits share a language that spoken word cannot communicate. It transcends the mind and speaks on the level of the spirit. It was, for some time, as if we were family; as if they had shared that journey with us and we with them. It's possible, through stories, to walk with someone on a journey that already was.

Remembering and reconnecting is so important. That's the point of Redeemer's instructions at His final Passover meal with His crew. He knew He was leaving, and He knew how important it would be for His followers to remember His life, death and rising. It was so important that He connected remembering to something as common as eating and drinking. We've formalized this remembering tool to a little cracker and a shot of juice, but it is so much more than that. Jesus said, "Whenever you eat and drink." Whenever you eat and drink. How often is that? When we eat together and drink together, we are to remember His life, death and rising.

Whenever you eat and drink, remember (to become a member with again; to join ourselves together with experiences by reflecting; to come into union (communion) with all that was by triggering images and words in our mind) me... remember me.

Frederick Buechner wrote in Secrets in the Dark that all humans share a common story and we share it with Christ. "Yet they meet as well as diverge, our stories and His, and even when they diverge, it is His they diverge

82

from, so that by His absence as well as by His presence in our lives we know who He is and who we are and who we are not. We have it in us to be Christ's to each other and maybe in some unimaginable way to God too—that's what we have to tell finally. We have it in us to work miracles of love and healing as well as to have them worked upon us. We have it in us to bless with Him and forgive with Him and heal with Him and once in a while maybe even to grieve with some measure of His grief at another's pain and to rejoice with some measure of His rejoicing at another's joy almost as if it were our own. And who knows but that in the end, by God's mercy, the two stories will converge for good and all, and though we would never have had the courage or the faith or the wit to die for Him any more than we have ever managed to live for Him very well either, His story will come true in us at last."

Remembering is so important. Just like with the Griesmers, it's as if they shared the journey with us and we with them.

Scott met Rebekah, the love of his life, in Lakeland and was soon married. The aching in Scott's bones for the story he found in Alaska burned in him until he and Rebekah decided to launch out and give Alaska a long term shot three years after his first trek. They loaded up all they could fit in their new rescue boat, an old Chevy Gladiator touring van, and took the trek across the wormhole to find themselves a few thousand miles from the safety and security of home.

Prior to leaving the safety of friends and family, Scott had secured a small cabin along the banks of the Little Su River in the wilderness of the Mat-Su Valley near Wasilla. Hoping to find employment on the other side, they were walking blind. Martin Luther King, Jr. once said that "faith is taking the first step when you can't see the whole staircase." This move was Scott's proverbial "step of faith."

Scott and Rebekah found employment at a department store, but the pay wasn't enough to sustain them. The following weeks were a dark cloud for Scott as he begged for guidance from the Maker. The rest is Scott's story to tell, but on one of those dark days in the valley, Scott took a stroll along the Little Su and desperately asked for direction from the Maker. After that little walk, they began to pack their belongings and prepare for the long trip home.

Whether the Maker whispered in his ear to move to Alaska or he just followed a selfish desire of his heart, or a little bit of both, he is still not sure. The adventure only lasted a couple of months, but the lessons he learned will last a lifetime. It took Scott a couple of years to dig out of the emotional hole he felt like he dug for his new little family, but as time passed, he was sure that he had become more of a man as a result.

It's perplexing when God takes something that we perceive as difficult and uses it to make us more who He meant us to be before the whole thing took place. The creative writer of those un-writable stories never fails to dream up the perfect endings! We may see a rabbit trail of life as a waste of time or a futile dead end, but to the Maker it is the only way we can get to where He's pointed us to go.

I read a story once, I think it was from the author C.S. Lewis, but I can't promise, who related a story of a man on the side of a mountain looking down at a cabin, his final destination for the night. As he peers off the cliff, which is impassible, he realizes that although he is, in proximity, very close to the cabin, he can't get there via the cliff. The distance between where he stands and the cabin is a closeness of proximity. But in order to arrive safely for the night he must take the "long" journey around the mountain, which is the closeness of approach. That trip to Alaska, for Scott, was the closest journey through which he could arrive at the final destination that God had for him. When things just don't seem to make sense, we must take into account the closeness of approach.

In his book on life as story, Donald Miller identifies the passageway from a good story to great. He learned that the difference in the two lies in the intensity of obstacles that one has to overcome in order to get to a desired end. His conclusion is that greater obstacles lead to richer stories. The greatest stories are those that have life and death obstacles. Maybe this explains why lives that tell a better story often include times of intense struggle. The most fulfilling marriages often have to walk through the darkest valley. *The Compass* says, "The testing of our faith produces endurance. And let endurance have its perfect result, so that you may be perfect and complete, lacking in nothing." James 1:2-4.

Maybe that is why we are instructed by the writer of the biblical book of James to embrace struggle.

Sticker Sales and Other New Beginnings

Early on in 1998, while Scott and I were still roommates at Southeastern, I pulled into the parking lot of the little church I was attending in Auburndale, Florida, and saw this young girl leaving in an old green Datsun hatchback. She threw her hand out of the window, which was manually rolled down with the old crank handle because it was central Florida and the car had no air conditioning, and waved like a flag blowing in gale force winds. It caught my attention and some number of months later, we were walking down the aisle at Grace Lutheran Church in Winter Haven, Florida.

Julie knew about my love and passion for Alaska. She never had it herself, but she loved me enough to sleepwalk in my dreams on occasion. If it meant anything to me, it meant everything to her.

In 1999, Julie had an opportunity to complete her college career at Southeastern with an internship at Focus on the Family in Colorado Springs. Everything was in place except for her housing for the five-week internship. "Let me call up Charles Bass," I said, excited to touch base with him again. Charles housed the gypsies three years ago in the basement of his Monument, Colorado home the night after the American Baptist pastor rescued us from being stranded a couple hours away.

"Of course we can help," Charles spoke with excitement over the phone.

So off Julie went within our first year of marriage to fulfill her five-week assignment and live in the basement of the Bass'.

Three weeks into her internship, I paid a visit to Julie and the Monument Hill crowd who hosted the gypsies a few years earlier. It was great to see everyone again. Nothing much had changed from our first visit. But everything would change before our next.

On night three of my visit with Julie and the Bass' we joined them for their nightly meal. Afterward, they began to ask us some pointed questions, "What are you planning to do when Julie graduates?"

We had no clue, we had not planned that far ahead yet, but I made up some stuff that sounded really good. When a man has no direction for his family, making up something comes natural.

After some more conversation, I began to share my dreams with Charles, "I really would like to start something new. I think I would like to be a part of starting a new church."

Starting new things had always been a passion of mine. In third grade I started a sticker business. I opened up my Corn Flakes that fateful Monday morning, poured them out in a big Pyrex bowl and cut the proof of purchase off the bottom of the box. I had collected my three cardboard treasures and they were ready to be stuck into a mailing envelope, addressed and rushed off to Corn Flakes headquarters. Two weeks later I received my box of four hundred stickers. It was one of those boxes with the stickers rolled inside so that you pull the tape out to reveal your next sticker. I used a few for myself and then began to imagine what I could do with the rest. "I could sell them, of course." My patience got the best of me as I waited for school to roll around the next day.

And there you have it; I started my first business, a third grade sticker empire. After the first batch from Corn Flakes HQ sold out, I purchased a collection of other stickers, a variety of shapes and subjects, masculine and feminine. I priced them according to size and appeal and began to turn a profit. Three days later I got a call to the principal's office. He shut down my first attempt to start an enterprise with the simple words, "You just can't sell things at school." I was devastated.

Some rivers run deep and the entrepreneurial bug bit me early!

Charles perked up with interest as I spoke of my desire to start a new church. It turned out that Monument Hill Church was sponsoring a new church start just a few miles up the road. "If you think you would really like to try it out, why don't you make the trip from

Lakeland to Monument more permanent and come help Randy and Terri Rankens with the new church?" Charles mused.

We agreed we would give it consideration and prayer until we could talk again in a few weeks. I caught the plane back to central Florida knowing deep inside that Julie and I were bound for Colorado in a few short months. The ride back home felt eerily similar to the fateful Monday morning third grade Kellogg's sticker revelation.

Different Kinds of Home

As the months passed, we agreed with Charles and Martha Bass that we would stay in their basement for a few weeks until we found jobs and a new place to live. In the meantime, Julie and I decided to take a little trip. It felt to me like I was returning home, not the home of my physical birth, but the home where something else was birthed in me.

Prior to 1996, I knew that there was a Maker, but I had no idea that he was big enough to create what I saw there. That birthed a new sense of wonder and fascination with Whoever it was that could create such other-worldly beauty and still come right down to our level and speak the language of the ARK02 and the Wormhole; the pivot point and the new shoes. That was an Artist that I wanted to know—we were going to ALASKA!

The plans were to stay on the Laverne Griffin Youth Camp for the month of June 2000 and then return to pack up our belongings and hop on another rescue boat, cargo hatch packed full of all our belongings, to Colorado to make a new home for ourselves. What a wonderful adventure our first year of marriage! We were even able to celebrate our first anniversary during our stay in Alaska.

Once again "what ifs" and "why nots" were the doorway to a new adventure.

This time around we took a plane to the Anchorage Airport where the Hales picked us up for Julie's first visit to the pivot point. Our stay there was somewhat uneventful: we cooked and cleaned, I played music and led short devotional times for the camp staff, we were able to see the camp full of activity, and we met several new friends from different parts of the country.

I began to embrace a new philosophy of home in the summer of 2000—home is not a place, but a web of relationships. Someone can own the most beautiful piece of property in a city, spend seven days a week there, and still not be home. There is a sense of comfort and security in knowing that you love and are loved: that wherever you are and whatever is happening is secondary to togetherness. That security is what I call home now. When we experience that in a place it is simply a window into our experience with the Maker, for He is the ultimate Home. One day we will be released from the walls that life has erected and we will run wild and free to His embrace as He lifts us high, smiles at us and says, "My son...my daughter...welcome Home."

Not So Lazy After All

Lazy Mountain...doesn't that sound like such a wonderful Sunday afternoon hiking destination?

We had been asking folks at the camp where to go for an afternoon hike. One of the staff members had a granddaughter in Anchorage who was willing to take us out for the day. She and her husband picked us up from the camp. Their chosen destination was a "little" hike up Lazy Mountain near the small town of Palmer. I had been looking forward to a hike like that since we arrived a couple weeks earlier.

I was a little concerned about Julie. We had been on a few hikes together and it was not her thing. I wondered if she would make it up the hill. I began to prepare myself for what lie ahead: helping my sweet wife survive when she couldn't help herself. I felt up for the task as we pulled into the little parking lot and put our small packs on our backs.

As we neared the trailhead we saw a man limping as he turned the corner and came from behind some bushes. He looked as if he was about to collapse. Turning to us he said,
"Damn, I sure as hell don't know why they call that thing lazy!"

It was that simple. After limping past us, he turned and walked away.

My mind raced with images of Julie falling and busting a knee and having to turn back early; maybe I would have to carry her down on my back and take her to the emergency room.

The couple who agreed to lead us up the hill were wonderful folks. He was a transplant from the lower forty-eight and she was Alaskan born and bred. She weighed about ninety pounds and I was also concerned for her on this trip. I remember thinking that if she was excited about this little hike, then it couldn't be too bad.

We continued on the trail and began to ascend the heights of Lazy Mountain. At one hundred yards in I began to breathe a little harder; five hundred yards I began to slow my pace. *Man, this first section is steep*, I thought as I began to struggle a bit. Julie seemed to be doing great. Why was I feeling a little winded? Maybe I was coming down with something.

The farther we climbed the harder it got to breathe. I was determined that I would not let the others know I was struggling. Skinny girl was laughing about some story her husband was telling. He was funny. I would have laughed too, but my lung would have collapsed. I felt sure the trail would level out soon.

It didn't.

I remember the point where every ounce of my concentration was on picking my left foot up and putting it above my right. I just wish that little skinny girl would stop asking questions, I thought. She didn't! My heart was beating about two hundred fifty beats per minute and my mind began to fade. I'm sure I was trying to answer skinny girl's questions, but I couldn't focus enough to even comprehend.

"Hey, can we take a break for just a minute?" I asked skinny girl who was bouncing up the hill in front of the rest of the group. And I asked again…and again.

Not me. I can't be the weak link! Not with skinny girl and my wife here. This can't happen.

Well, it happened and I was humiliated. We reached a little platform an hour or so into our hike and I had to ask everyone to turn back. Skinny girl and all!

Sometimes I have an elevated view of myself. I've always been an optimist, expecting things to be much easier and myself to be much more qualified than I really am. Humility is the perfect pill for that disease. Isn't it awakening to realize you're mortal? Isn't it good to know that we are not super-humans? Isn't it freedom to be able to dive headlong into the sufficiency of Redeemer!

Lazy Mountain kicked my butt…and so did skinny girl!

As I've hiked more and more in Alaska over the years, I've realized that the physical part is a mind game. I've watched guys that can run a marathon struggle with equal intensity as the couch monkey. It really doesn't matter who you are, your first trip out in Alaska is going to kick your butt! And then you realize that it is your mind playing tricks on you, not your body. I think that's true with most of life. We are all much stronger and much weaker than we imagine. It's in sorting out that dichotomy that we find our true strength.

An Urgent Request

Later that afternoon, I was able to get past my failure on Lazy Mountain and get back to work at the camp. As I made my way around the camp, I thought often of some of my best friends, Kevin and Sonya Yates. The Yates had been through some tough times as of late. They were discouraged and confused about their future. I could not stop thinking about them and I began to wonder if they should be with us for a while this summer at the Pivot Point. Were they meant to share in this better story we were discovering? Would they find a new "home" there?

One morning I was preparing the devotional for the camp staff and I was sure of it: the Yates were meant to be in Alaska in June of 2000. I shared this with the camp staff at devotion and how it would be impossible unless the Maker provided the resources for the trip. Much to my surprise, one of the men around the circle spoke up and said something like, "That's no problem, if they are supposed to be here, money is no problem."

A week or so later, after many phone calls and pleas to come, the Yates arrived at the Ted Stevens Airport in Anchorage ready to take the same drive north that Julie and I took just a dozen or so days earlier. I do not fully understand how the Maker whispers in our ear, but it became obvious over the next few days that I had heard him loud and clear. Somehow release came for those prisoners caged by the worries of life. I watched it in their eyes. I heard it in their prayers. I felt it in their embrace. The hard places softened and the soft places began to mend.

When people spend a week in the isolation of a less civilized place, they think about things that the busyness of life crowds out. A few days in, your heart begins to soften. Your mind begins to open doors of spaces that have been shut for years. The dead places begin to come back to life. The problems that seem so pressing in "the real world" seem so much less so in the absence of urgency. Life simplifies and hearts mend. Perspective expands.

A week later, the Yates left the pivot point headed in a new direction. They founded a small non-profit organization called Beyond Walls and would return several times in the years following their first visit. They hauled food into poverty-stricken villages and hosted sports camps to try to provide those living in the rigorous Alaskan climate and conditions with relief in the name of the Maker.

Our relationship with the Yates has been off and on for the past twelve years, but I would not trade that silent moment when the Maker spoke on behalf of two fellow pilgrims for anything in the world; it is part of my story as much as it is part of theirs. It is exhilarating to sit back and watch how the Maker weaves the stories together into a beautiful tapestry of love and life which will be on display long after the flames of this walk darken into lightly glowing embers carried on by our children and grandchildren. A plurality of stories becomes one as the curtain rises to reveal the overarching plot and the hero, whose name is Redeemer.

A Celebration to Remember

"Gratitude unlocks the fullness of life. It turns what we have into enough, and more. It turns denial into acceptance, chaos to order, and confusion to clarity. It can turn a meal into a feast, a house into a home, a stranger into a friend." - Melody Beattie[8]

"We are celebrating the feast of the Eternal Birth which God the Father has borne and never ceases to bear in all eternity...But if it takes not place in me, what avails it? Everything lies in this, that it should take place in me." - Meister Eckhart

"Go out to the roads and country lanes and compel them to come in, so that my house will be full." – Jesus, *The Compass,* Luke 14:23

It was our one-year anniversary.

June 25th, 2000, was a day that I will never forget and it even came complete with the top layer of our wedding cake. What better place for Julie and me to celebrate our first year of marriage than south-central Alaska? What a gift our friends at the camp gave us by loaning us a vehicle to take a trip south and east. After a short visit to the glacier upon which the gypsies danced, we drove to a ski resort called Alyeska a few miles east of Anchorage and spent the night in a wonderful bed and breakfast before we headed south to the Kenai Peninsula.

I'll never forget that night in the bed and breakfast when we broke open the duct tape that held together the box that protected the top layer of our wedding cake. We had lugged it all the way from central Florida just for this occasion. We pulled it from the little six-pack cooler that we had lined with ice to try to keep the icing from melting away. We cut a piece and ate as if it were the day we sealed the deal with a kiss in front of all those people. I can't say the cake was tasty, but the memories were fabulous. We revisited all the events of our wedding day, one year earlier. Memorials help us maintain our passion for life. Not every day is a memory maker. Most days of our lives are laced with things we hope to forget. "Stones of Remembrance" remind us that there are a few unforgettable experiences in life that make all the others worth it.

I had never seen such lush green vegetation as the trip to the coast. Several times we stopped the car to stare into the lush fields of wildflowers adorned with the promise of spring. The smell of newness and rebirth wafted through the air like a tuft of smoke from a sailor's pipe. The Alaskan wildlife was spectacular: from mountain goats hanging off cliffs to moose hanging out in meadows. The drive was simply a gift to help us discover what God had given us in this journey called marriage.

I think that marriage is not the point. Young folks often feel that life will be different when they walk the aisle and kiss the bride. We think that all of our problems will vanish. We feel that the hungers of the flesh will be satisfied. We expect that happily ever after is the end of the story.

But it's not!

Marriage is beautiful for sure, but the beauty is not in the absence of pain. It's not the relief of satisfied loneliness. No...marriage is just another step in the journey. Like so many other aspects of life, it is a pathway to a deeper level of maturity. *The Compass* traces the life of a man named Paul. When it came to marriage, he spoke of the beauty of mutual submission and sacrifice, and then he made a peculiar observation: the mystery of marriage is great, and then he pronounced, "But I am speaking with reference to Christ and the Church."

Wow! The gorgeous scenery of marriage is simply a book to be read about life with Redeemer...

The lush vegetation and the dangerous wildlife, the rocky terrain and the winding roads are simply a metaphor. An earthly marriage relationship is like the relationship between Redeemer and the Church. Christ sacrificed for His people and His people honor Him as their Lord. As a husband and wife must work in relationship with one another, so the Redeemer walks with us.

I believe that all good things in life simply reflect some aspect of life with Redeemer. The God who set the galaxies in motion is intentional with every single detail of every single life. If every good gift were not given, we would know less about the character of the Maker. He loves us enough to infuse our understanding of Him with "happily ever after." That's the point of good stories—they all have the same characteristics simply because they all point to Him, and because He is the ultimate good, we find Him revealed in good stories.

So marriage is a visual aid, of sorts, for life with Redeemer.

Now, don't get me wrong, we screw our good stories up royally. Our selfishness and greed, un-forgiveness and pain make up the wrecking ball that demolishes His temple of love in our lives. He loved us enough to allow us to crash His party. If we had no choice in love, what would it mean? It would have no power if we were forced into submission. Millions of folks around the world must think: if relationship with God is like my marriage, then He can have it, I'm moving on. But it wasn't like that in the beginning, before we hurt one another and before our selfishness and pride cut so deeply into the relationship we share.

If you have been married before, you know exactly what I mean. When I officiate at wedding ceremonies, my favorite moment is when the bride makes her appearance. I feel so honored to be standing side by side with the groom. I always watch his face when the bride appears at the end of the aisle. It is full of "what ifs" and "why nots." Tears well up in his eyes and he just begins to lose his cool. His perfect bride making her way across a crowded room to present herself as his forever! Yes, forever! No one gets married expecting to part ways down the road. It's just not in our hearts to do that. That story is way too small for what that the Maker put in us. The bride and groom have faith in one another. They simply believe. They make a verbal agreement to forever.

Enter selfishness. He is a bastard child of the flesh. And he doesn't partner well with sacrifice and forgiveness. He fights a tough fight, and he often wins: violently taking down the soldier of promise; taking commitment as a prisoner of war, and stripping us of the glory of the relationship that parallels that of Christ and the Church.

He creatively confuses us about Who Redeemer claims to be. The antagonist of our souls successfully takes from us the one visual aid God designed to help us understand how much Redeemer cares and how permanent His love for us is: marriage.

That trip south and east was an opportunity to peer deeply through the window of what love is meant to be. I am always thankful when I travel to a place that looks exactly as it looked a thousand years before. It is simply a portrait of the unchanging God who loves us now and forevermore. And it is a reminder of what life was before we polluted it with selfishness and greed.

Seward

When we arrived at the docks, bald eagles soared everywhere overhead; sea otters rolled and backpedaled while thousands of sockeye salmon swam up the streams shoulder to shoulder and nose to tail; the halibut hung like overcoats from the makeshift meat hooks; and men stood along the docks filleting fish with the speed and precision of Olympic sprinters jumping hurdles.

We hopped on a boat for a short trip through the Kenai Fjords to see animals I had only dreamt of prior. Puffins were fluttering their wings as they tried to cling to the sharp rock walls. The beluga whales were teasing us with the graceful dance of their tales arching over the surface of the water. The sea lions were playing and bathing in the sun in their tight-knit community habitat. My camera shutter must have looked like the wings of a hummingbird as I recorded to film what I thought may be a once-in-a-lifetime experience.

The uniqueness and beauty of it all seemed to simply be a Polaroid of the life Julie and I would live together in the most sacred promise a man and woman could make to one another. Marriage is filled with beauty, abundance, tension, color and even danger. Some days are painted with neutral tones while others are colored with the boldness of the primaries. Some seasons are songs written in the somber minor keys, while others sound like the playfulness of circus music. We run across friend and foe, victory and defeat, life and death. Every day is different and that is the beauty of it all. As singer/songwriter Andrew Peterson writes, it is like "dancing in the minefields, sailing in the storms. It was harder than we dreamed, but I believe that's what the promise is for."

In the toughest times of life and marriage, my heart and soul often have to take a back seat to another character in our story. The Spirit within me soars above all of our circumstances and situations and watches as my mind and will do their thing. When logic and emotion fail or flounder, the Eagle has to swoop in and take charge. For within my spirit rests an ability to make decisions independently of my mind and emotion. The spirit is a gift from the Maker, the greatest gift of all, in fact. For it is by the work of the spirit that love finds its way. Often, love is a willful decision that makes no sense to the mind and does not feel good to emotion. If we remove the spirit, we forfeit the power of the unconditional nature of authentic love. I embrace the mind and appreciate emotion, but when all else fails, let the spirit soar!

Julie and I threw down blankets beside the shores of the Kenai Fjords in front of the little camper trailer we borrowed from the Hales. As we sat there, a pitter-patter of rain began to fall. I remember looking at her and reveling in the fact that she was mine forever; that we were His forever. As the rain began to fall harder, we made our way back into the little camper trailer, cuddled up in that cozy little bed and slept soundly in anticipation of what the Maker had planned for the remainder of our lives.

Fulfilling Our Duties on the Pivot Point

The Family Feast

When we arrived back at the camp the following day, we had quite the surprise waiting for us. That particular week in June, five couples staying at the Pivot Point had wedding anniversaries. Sunday afternoon all of those couples, and others from the surrounding community, contributed to a celebration feast that will rest in my memory for a lifetime. Moose cooked several different ways, caribou steaks, Alaskan king crab legs, beer battered halibut, red salmon, fresh prawns and other wild game adorned the kitchen at the camp where we ate and laughed the night away in celebration of marriage and community. I remember having to tear myself away at the end of the night...I wanted it to last forever.

No thanksgiving meal has ever meant more to me than that experience. I cannot even tell you the names of most of the people there that night, but we were family! Experiences such as these transcend unfamiliar relationships and allow us to peer into our future together in eternity with the Maker and His children. We will know others as they were meant to be and we will be known with a transparency that will set us free from any inhibitions that hold us back from true authentic relationship with our fellow pilgrims on the journey of life.

Over the next week we were given another gift that set our hearts free. We took a drive with the Hales to see more of Alaska. My heart raced as we watched a brown bear nurture her baby twin cubs in Denali. I will forever cherish the excitement as I inched closer and closer to that bull moose as he ducked his head under the water of the river and rose up with huge blades of grass hanging from his velvety rack just twenty feet away as I hid in the brush in Fairbanks. And I still laugh when I remember posing for a picture underneath the huge sign that read "First Baptist Church of North Pole" and saying to Julie, "There really is a First Baptist Church in every city in North America."

The memory of the ribs cooked on an open flame by native Alaskans in who knows where with our new best friends still fills my empty soul. This, my second trip to Alaska, took me deeper into the heart of the Maker and caused my heart to leap one notch higher as I shared this precious place with my treasured bride.

This experience happened only four years after the visit with the gypsies. However, I experienced the first as a boy and the second as a man. So much happened in that four years in between and I was a different person: less innocent, yet more pure. We grow quickly and think we have come so far. Then every year following holds more opportunities to grow and learn; to change and become new all over again.

That was our last visit to the Pivot Point. The Hales have moved on as well. I recently visited the Pivot Point and found a new camp: one filled with new people having new experiences no less wonderful and no more unique than ours. But it was not be the same place. Everything had changed—it morphed into its next stage of life. And we cannot look back hoping for what was. We must put one foot in front of the other waiting with anticipation for what will be. It is the future that offers us a hope for more, because the Maker takes us deeper into His heart and His plan for our lives.

There really is a North Pole, Alaska!

My New Friend

After our return home in 2000, our faith family at Crossroads, the little gathering place in Florida where I first saw Julie's arm waving in the breeze, helped us load up the moving van and we were off across the country for another adventure. Julie and I moved to central Colorado and we were part of starting that new church for two years. Julie did not develop the same passion for Alaska that I found with the gypsies. Otherwise, I may have made a premature decision to move there permanently and, in hindsight, miss all that God had for us in Colorado, Florida and Alabama in the years to follow.

Our Colorado experience was difficult in many ways. The relationships we developed there were stressful and Julie and I were challenged by our first two years of life together. The journey of a woman learning to live with a man and vice versa is a monster all by itself. When you add a move to a place where you know no one and are a couple thousand miles from family, it is even harder.

We had the purest of intentions there. We dreamed of a church that would grow and become a beacon of light for the community, and we invested deeply into the people there, and we placed ourselves in a vulnerable position and when things went south, it hurt. I'm sure we weren't the only ones hurt; I think the whole thing just hurt.

Isn't it interesting how people with pure hearts and shared motives, the ones who love the Maker and believe the best about one another, can begin to question each other? Trust sometimes seems to wax and wane. We forget so easily what we've been through together.

We are closest to those people who are family, whether in our genealogical family or faith family. We have such a strong tie with those folks that it hurts terribly when the rope breaks. Our motives and vision are so intertwined that the least unraveling will make it all fall apart. That's kind of what we experienced in Colorado. We had such a close relationship with so many people, but we failed to establish trust.

That little church has come and gone and in many ways it left behind a trail of tears laced with a spattering of joy. In the midst of all of that, relationships were born. Some of those died; others will remain. In our youth, inexperience and lack of wisdom we wallowed in the pit of self-pity and were almost buried emotionally in the foothills of the Rockies.

Others hurt too. Sometimes it seems like such an indulgent waste of youth, then I remember the fruit. Dave and Kelsey...Red and Kim...when it seems like we've done little, the Maker causes the mustard seed to grow into the largest tree in the garden. We must remember that the whole thing is not about us or about our feelings and experiences; it is about others coming to know the Love of the Maker. We can only hope that our name will be brought low and His lifted high!

Scott and Rebekah moved west to help us with that project. It was so good to be with them again, but even that relationship seemed to be different...distant. It was time to move on. We went back for a visit a couple years ago. Just like the pivot point, we realized that we can't go back to visit the past…it's not there. Although we found the same people and the same places, time had marched on and what we followed there to pursue was left behind.

After our initial commitment to Colorado waned, we moved back to central Florida, where we had our first child. Eighteen months later we were off again to settle in to the rest of our lives in east Alabama at the Maker's beckoning call. Since then we have had three more children and we both feel like where we live is home for our little family. Although it took us a few years to settle down here, it was worth the journey as we experienced new adventures at every stop.

Having settled in to a new experience of life, Alaska became simply an intriguing story from a past life. I occasionally remembered my commitment twelve years earlier to get as many men there as possible to make room in their life to experience what I experienced. But, the pressures of life convinced me that the Alaska story might be over, or at best a twinkle in my eye that may be fanned into flame after children are out of college and Julie and I settle in as empty nesters.

I was doing life in November 2007. We had started a new faith community in Auburn, which was meeting on Sunday nights. A young man walked into the historic home in downtown where we were gathering and sat quietly around a small table outside of the room where I was teaching. He was a handsome man who had a fire in his eyes and a smile that drew you deeply into his personality. His demeanor was quiet, but his passion was loud. The room seemed to light up when Peter walked through the door. It was so obvious how much he loved people, and I needed to get to know that man. Little did I know, Peter Goodwin would become a catalyst in my life for yet another transformation and more trips to the place where the journey began twelve years earlier.

Let me give you a little back story.

A generation before I met Peter, his dad, Mark, was wrestling with the transition from boyhood to man. He graduated high school, loaded his car and took off for college unsure of why. When he arrived on campus in another southeastern state, he couldn't find a parking spot. Dazed and confused with passion in his eyes and fire in his belly he kept on driving, chasing his own adventures and looking for answers to his boyhood questions. Heading west and then north, he made his own journey through the wormhole and didn't stop until he arrived at a pivot point of his own in south-central Alaska.

Who knows why young men do what they do? Part of the beauty of being young is that we were not afraid to follow our hearts wherever they led and at whatever the cost; Mark did just that. He found himself a new home and bumped into the lady with which he would choose to spend the rest of his life.

Although Peter didn't spend his childhood living in Alaska, he spent most of his summers there wandering around the Alaskan bush with Uncle John, his mother's older brother. Uncle John was the typical man's man; *John Wayne* they call him. No boy could imagine more adventure than Peter experienced touring the backcountry with Uncle John in bush planes, fishing the pristine streams of southern Alaska and shooting wild animals in a place far from home. Fish, wild animals and tough terrain began to prepare him for a future leading people deep into the wilderness of Alaska.

Somehow Peter ended up living in Auburn. Ready to start a new life with his future bride, and looking for the

110

next step in his life, he found himself sitting at that dining table among the faith community meeting in the historic home that Sunday night in November of 2007.

The Walls Came Tumbling Down

Although Peter and I met a time or two to discuss his passion to take men on wilderness journeys to Alaska, our relationship was put on hold for a couple months while the walls of my life came tumbling down. As I look back on Peter's arrival on this scene of my life, I can't express the awe I feel as I realize that the Maker sent Peter as a gift that would help stabilize me when everything in my life was crumbling. If not Peter, the Maker would have sent another hero, but Peter was available and the Redeemer chose him.

Our faith community was gathered to share a meal together the Sunday night before Thanksgiving. I bowed to pray over our evening and began to thank the Maker for the new family He had given me over the past year. I finished the prayer with no idea that the family I just mentioned would become a source of support and strength carrying me through the grueling months to come. When I opened my eyes, everything changed. EVERYTHING.

The year leading up to this night was one of the most challenging of my life. I had traveled to Lakeland, Florida to complete a Master's degree at Southeastern one week of each of the preceding ten months. Our house had been on the market for months with almost a dozen offers falling through after the housing market crashed earlier that year. We had finally sold and closed on a house and the following day we were to move all of our belongings across town to settle into our new home. In addition to the stress of starting a new faith community, school and the move, Julie was eight months pregnant with our third child.

That's when I found myself praying that night. Melanie, my cousin who moved to Auburn to help us with our new venture, walked in the door, "Kevin, I've got to talk with you alone. Julie, you too." The intensity in her voice let us know that all was not well. We walked into a little room as Melanie began, "Kevin, it's your dad. He was on his way here and he had an accident. He didn't make it."

Julie began to cry and I just sunk to the ground with a blank stare and no emotion to walk me through this tragic moment. In later days I would have a terrible sense of guilt that I didn't feel anything. I assume it was some level of shock, but I didn't understand why my emotions would not catch up with the reality that I was faced with that Thanksgiving week of 2007.

We took our two children to a friend's house, made some quick last-minute plans for the move the following day and headed three and a half hours north to begin the grieving process and plan the funeral for my dad. You cannot imagine what one goes through in a situation like this until you have experienced it yourself. The emotional pain of the experience coupled with the quick planning and overwhelming details of what to do next was almost more than I could bear. We stopped by the hospital and picked up my dad's personal belongings and then made the trip north.

I'll never forget sticking my hand down in that large manila envelope in the hospital waiting room that night and pulling out my dad's stuff. It was as if another hand reached down and squeezed my heart until it burst. It was the first tangible reality check that my dad was gone. The grief felt like a darkness deep enough to drown in. I pulled out his wallet, his identification, his glasses, and some other personal items. It began a long process of transference. Although it was just stuff, it felt like his paternal covering, with all its glory and flaws, passed on to me that night. I felt like a man for the first time…and it was terrifying. No longer would this rescue me. No more would I be able to fall back on my protector. I was alone now…so alone. It would take me some time to learn how to lean on my heavenly father. I was crushed.

Death feels like such an end. In the midst of the grief it feels like life is over, never to be revisited. But the truth is it has only begun.

"This is not the end here at this grave
This is just a hole that someone made
Every hole was made to fill
And every heart can feel it still--
Our nature hates a vacuum
This is not the hardest part of all
This is just the seed that has to fall
All our lives we till the ground
Until we lay our sorrows down
And watch the sky for rain
There is more
More than all this pain
More than all the falling down
And the getting up again
There is more
More than we can see
From our tiny vantage point
In this vast eternity
There is more
A thing resounds when it rings true
Ringing all the bells inside of you
Like a golden sky on a summer eve
Your heart is tugging at your sleeve
And you cannot say why
There must be more
There is more
More than we can stand
Standing in the glory
Of a love that never ends
There is more
More than we can guess
More and more, forever more
And not a second less
There is more than what the naked eye can see
Clothing all our days with mystery
Watching over everything
Wilder than our wildest dreams
Could ever dream to be
There is more"
- Andrew Peterson and Pierce Pettis, "More"[9]

We buried my dad that cool November afternoon and all my friends and family were there to see him off. Scott, the gypsy, spoke at his funeral. There's so much comfort in knowing that those closest to you are there in those times to wrap their arms around you and love on you: tangible expressions of God's promise for peace in the midst of chaos.

Two weeks later, I traveled to central Florida to turn in my thesis and walk the graduation aisle. Two weeks after that, Julie delivered our third child, Kenneth Daniel. My dad's name was Kenneth, but he went by his middle name. My boy carried a bit of my dad forward to ease the pain. For six months the fog of war did not lift as I wallowed in the mire of self-pity and self-focus. Julie was a hero through this experience. Although our marriage struggled over the next year, Julie's heroism during the months following dad's death was remarkable. I am so proud of her.

When we returned to Auburn with most of my father's belongings in tow a few days later, I had no idea how to start the healing process. I felt out of place everywhere I went. Our immediate family felt different, our faith family felt different, the people on the street even looked different. There seemed to be no familiar place to rest.

Although dozens of friends worked hard to console me in my struggles, it was Peter who seemed to bring peace to the turmoil in my soul. I still do not know why, but when I would sit with Peter in the cab of his truck, or sit across the table as we shared lunch together, something inside me calmed. Maybe it was that Peter had experienced similar struggles and had some insight into what I needed to hear, which was mostly nothing at all. Whatever the reason, my relationship with Peter was one of the only sources of solace in the chaos of tragedy.

There were others who served to bring order to the chaos. Bethany and Dave, who had been with us for two years, were also a source of peace. Daniel, our newest baby, brought joy to us as his new life began to fill the void of the life that had passed. There were so many others who cared enough to simply love us through the hard times and expect nothing in return.

Within a few weeks, my friendship with Peter felt like it had been a life-long experience. Peter would share stories of Alaska and what he learned about men as they hunted big game together. He began to share a dream; he had to take men, who did not have the resources to experience Alaska, on tours of the Bush. As I listened, my heart leapt with anticipation of how I could plug into the dream that the Maker had given to Peter and how it might converge with my commitment a decade earlier to take as many men as I could to experience what the Maker had to offer there.

Peter had no idea what was going on inside my head and he had little knowledge of my experience eleven years earlier with the gypsies. He also had no idea that the Maker sent him to me at the perfect time to offer hope in hopelessness, which would prove to be another wormhole in the story of my life. If he had known the importance of his presence, he would have been able to claim he had something to offer. Instead, the Maker just gently handed him over as a new best friend and allowed me to realize all over again that only God could write a story such as this.

We were sitting outside a local BBQ restaurant in Auburn when Peter had just shared that he felt like it was time for him to take a small group of men into the Alaskan bush for a week together in the wilderness. I looked Peter in the eye and said, "Do you think I could go with you?" He was surprised by my question. I had butterflies in my stomach as the words rolled off my tongue. What if he didn't think I had what it takes?

"Would you want to go?" He asked.

"It would be a dream come true," I replied.

"Heck, yeah!"

Right there in the cab of that pick-up truck in the parking lot of Byron's Smokehouse, a baby was born. Original Design Outfitters, later to become Alaskan Ventures, would be a dream come true for Peter. And I became, not only a mid-wife to that baby as I asked probing questions in the months to come, but a tag-along who barely had strength to lift his head off his pillow at the start of each new day.

A few months later, the last week of July 2008, I hopped on an airplane on my way to the place of the memories of twelve years earlier and a fire in my belly that all the water in Alabama could not put out. Once again I was "Alaska or Bust." These are the words I wrote on the plane as I traveled to this next adventure:

"I can't believe I am on a plane and my next stop is Anchorage! I haven't been to Alaska since Julie and I spent June of 2000 there. 2007 was almost more than I could deal with. Now I'm unplugging from it all for twelve days. The hardest to deal with is that it is because of the climax and the weight of last year that I am even able to do this. I really have no clue how all that works together, but I grasp more than ever before...actually I grasp for the first time...how "'all things work together.'" I am revisiting my perspective of God's hand in all our circumstances. I have no clue just how involved He is in our lives. Sometimes I think He has designed an overarching blueprint of rewards and consequences and left us with it and sometimes it seems His hand is in almost every circumstance.

Maybe it is both...

The following days are going to be very challenging. God began weeks (maybe months) ago penetrating my heart for this. I am completely drained and running on empty. I need some fuel. I need restoration in vision. I need deliverance from me. I need the Holy Spirit."

"God blesses (gives the gift of joy) those who are poor and realize their need for Him. For theirs is the Kingdom of Heaven. God blesses those who mourn. For they will be comforted. God blesses those who are humble. For they will inherit the Earth. God blesses those who hunger and thirst for justice. For they will be satisfied. God blesses those who are merciful. For they will be shown mercy. God blesses those whose hearts are pure. For they will see God. God blesses those who work for peace. For they will be called children of God. God blesses those who are persecuted for doing right. For the Kingdom of Heaven is theirs." Matthew 5:3-10 NLT.

I was poor in spirit. I realized there was nothing else I could do without Him. He took me back to where it all began.

Loosening the Grip of Grief

"I believe that divine love, incarnate and indwelling in the world, summons the world always toward wholeness, which ultimately is reconciliation and atonement with God."
- Wendell Berry[10]

"Now the wren has gone to roost and the sky is turnin' gold And like the sky my soul is also turning 'Turnin' from the past, at last and all I've left behind." - Ray LaMontagne and the Pariah Dogs[11]

"The difference between truth and fiction is that fiction has to make sense." - Mark Twain

It had been nine months since the tragic day in November when my dad passed from this life onward. The first six months following his accident I crashed: about twelve sessions of marriage counseling had kept my marriage afloat. Our family was learning to live with three children, while I was learning to live without the safety net of my dad who had bailed me out of so many self-manufactured problems in the years leading up to then. Just as the first Alaska trip was a step from boyhood to man, my dad's passing was another leap toward manhood. I was becoming a foundation instead of the building resting upon it. When a man's father

119

passes, it forces him into a new level of manhood, as the one leaning on a rock becomes the rock upon which others lean. The big question on my mind was "Am I ready for such a leap?"

We were expecting six pilgrims on this first trek as Original Design Outfitters. Peter, his dad, Mark, and I would join three others from California: Mike, Damon and Jeremy.

Peter grew up spending his summers in Alaska and Mark spent several years of his life living there. It was my third visit to Alaska and my first to the bush. The other three were making their first.

The plan was for Peter and me to fly into Anchorage, spend the night with Peter's uncle Nate, shop for supplies the following day, and then catch a bush plane to Port Alsworth about two hundred twenty miles by air from Anchorage.

My biggest fear of being in the wilderness of Alaska was a lack of sleep. I am not much of a sleeper in the most comfortable of situations; I had no idea how I would sleep in the Alaskan wilderness.

Peter wanted us to pack as lightly as possible on that first trip; he and I didn't carry tents, instead we packed bivy bags. Bivies are used in military survival scenarios and are basically the equivalent of body bags. They are a waterproof, breathable outer skin that houses your sleeping bag and acts as a tent, but is shaped like the bag itself. I thought I would be able to handle that, but would I be able to endure being zipped up inside of the "body bag" if it were to rain? I am terrified of tight spaces; some call it claustrophobia, I call it hell. And how would I handle the fear of being in the vulnerable open-air sleeping scenario in an area highly populated with bear and moose?

As I was sleeping at Nate's house that first night in Anchorage, I asked that the Maker would be with me as we made our journey through the bush. I pulled out my Bible, *The Compass*, and these are the words I jotted down in my journal:

"I am scared to death that I will not sleep for the next 10 days."

"I lay down and sleep, yet I woke up in safety, for the Lord was watching over me...I am not afraid of 10,000 enemies who surround me on every side." Psalm 3:5-6.

"In peace I will lie down and sleep, for you alone, oh Lord, will keep me safe." Psalm 4:8.

"When I look at the night sky and see the work of your fingers—the moon and the stars you set in place—what are mere mortals that you should think about them? Human beings that you should think about them?" Psalm 8:3-4.

"You can go to bed without fear. You will lie down and sleep soundly. You need not be afraid of sudden disaster or destruction that comes to the wicked, for the Lord is your security." Proverbs 3:24-25.

These arrows in my "compass" rested in my mind and heart for the next ten days as we made our way through the Alaskan wilderness. It's funny how the thing that scares us most is the fear of being afraid. I was quite sure that we would not be attacked by a grizzly or trampled a moose, but the thought of waking up in the night to face one staring at me scared me the most. That's how the antagonist works; he intimidates us with intimidation itself. His strategy is not to make us afraid of dying, but to make us afraid of being afraid of dying. He is a sly fox; a strategic genius.

A Morning I Will Not Soon Forget

Grief had been gripping me for about eight months. John Sewell, my counselor, warned me that the grief cycle lasts about two years. He said there would be times when we took huge steps toward normalcy and there would be other times when I would feel like I was bouncing off walls of emotions including anger, fear, hopelessness, confusion and others. He was right. But the morning of July 25th, 2008, was one of those "big step" mornings.

Up to this point in my Alaskan experiences, I loved Alaska as a childhood best friend. It was safe and secure. It was once a raging wilderness both dangerous and wild, but had since been tamed by the people who sacrificed to make their way there to domesticate it and make it a safe, fun place for me to visit. I loved it like we often love the Sunday School Jesus, our playmate on the church playground.

I had heard Peter's story of the nights stuck on the mountain in below freezing temperatures with sleet and sixty miles-per-hour winds. Those stories were intriguing but not a reality to me. It is similar to how we can be so comfortable in our church buildings. Throughout the centuries noble men and women have suffered a brutal death as they stood up for their faith in Redeemer. Now we sit comfortable in the proverbial padded pews of our faith riding on the backs of their sacrifice. We are arrogant enough to sleep comfortably in the bed that those that went before us carved out with their sacrifice. Now I would look in the faces of the men and women who are still cutting roads through the wilderness of the front lines and I would be challenged.

Peter, Nate and I gathered at a little breakfast restaurant to talk about our life and faith. The three of us sat across a table from each other sharing stories that would change not only my perspective of Alaska, but also my perspective of life. The gracious silent whisper of the Maker would once again shout in my ear and

122

shake me with the reality of who He is and who I am.

In moments when we gain this perspective, things change. Sitting at that table, my heart began to soften, the fallow ground was broken up and I received the seed of healing that would grow and blossom into the fruit of redemption of the experiences of the last year. I was beckoned to the front lines. It was not the front lines of Alaska, but the front lines of my walk of faith.

We each shared our own stories. I shared my story of losing my dad and the other experiences of 2007 that rocked my safe world. And then I just sat and listened for a couple of hours to the stories that sent my heart on a new journey: a journey of hope and freedom from the pain I had experienced.

Peter told of the night he was guiding a hunt in which the hunter became the hunted. It was on a brown bear hunt in southwest Alaska a few years before. He and his hunter had injured the bear and had to shift from the mindset of the predator to the prey, while still trying to finish off the hulk of a bear. After a long evening, they were the final victor in this battle between man and beast. The problem was that it was too late to return to camp. They had to spend the night in the freezing weather shaking like a leaf as they were on the edge of hypothermia. Their only means of warmth and protection from the elements was the skin of the animal they had just slain. They slept inside the hide of the bear and that bloody mess became their ARK02, yet another rescue boat in this story of adventure. The trophy that represented their victory became the provision for their survival from the weather of the wilderness to which they voluntarily submitted themselves in order to take control over the wild.

That's one reason why men hunt in a modern world with all the food we need around the corner at the local grocery store—we hunt to feel power. We hunt to have some experience of control over the wilderness. The Maker made us superior to the beasts of the field and we feel like we are living out our destiny when we win a victory over the wild. We expect an experience like this to change us; to make us more of a man. But what we discover is that the greatest change happens when the Maker reveals our weaknesses to us. When the fragility of life reveals itself and we feel small. That feeling of humility enhances our reliance on the Maker and forces us to cling to the true source of Life. Any other experience is just an impostor of what we were made to know, that God loves and trusts us enough to send us to the front lines.

Safety and security serves as our crutch to compensate for the brokenness of our souls. Peter watched as a helpless spectator as God revealed the other side of His personality to this man who got more than he bargained for on the side of that cold mountain. God is the God of peace and love, but He is also the dangerous and fierce God of *The Compass*. We are to love Him, we are to rest in His safety, but we are also called to step over the cliff of radical pursuit of Him even if it leads us into a minefield through which we are tip-toeing, hoping for the best as He directs our every step, zigzagging through potential disaster as we carry a fellow soldier to safety on the shoulders of faith. He is the rescuer, the hero, and we are simply His hands and feet.

The Maker cared enough to send his only Son into what seemed to be the most tragic defeat in history and He cares enough to send us, members of his body here on Earth, into that same level of risk in order to rescue the lost pilgrim on the dark side of the mountain. This is the God we are honored to serve!

After Peter finished his story, Nate began to share a story that changed my life forever. It was one of those rare moments when simple words are translated into arrows that penetrate the hard outer surface of our heart before digging deep and transforming us into someone different, someone more alive and free. That story will stay etched deeply into the heart of who I am for eternity. It is a story of a terrible tragedy. I wish it had never happened, but at the same time I am deeply grateful that God is continuing to redeem it and use it in people like me.

It had been three years since Nate lost three nieces. Samantha, Jesse and Katherine Davis were ages nine, seven, and five.

The three girls lived in a small village called Port Alsworth on the shores of Lake Clark and the national park that bears its name. They lived in an isolated community with their mother and father, Michelle and Jeremy and their three brothers, Jack, Callen and Taylor. When anyone loses three nieces it obviously means that two parents lost three children.

Living in the bush in Alaska means that your mode of transportation shifts from cars and SUVs to bush planes—they are a way of life, not a luxury. Along with air transportation come plane crashes, and I learned that there are a lot of them. In comparison to the number of flights, crashes are few and far between, but a plane crash is a plane crash.

Jeremy, Michelle and their three girls were making a routine trip into the city in their small bush plane, something that happens quite often. One of the many uncontrollable aspects of Alaska is the weather. It can turn on a dime. On this particular day, just minutes from home, this young family was caught in a whiteout blizzard that came from nowhere, and came quickly.

As Jeremy, who currently has thousands of hours in the air, tried to find a place to bring the plane down he thought he was coming out of it and found the plane skidding on its belly along the frozen lake. It seemed they would skid to a complete stop without too much harm and then the tragedy began.

The ice broke and the plane plunged into nine hundred feet of icy waters. Jeremy is experienced enough in situations such as these to stay calm. While under thirty feet of water, he grabbed for his knife to cut his seatbelt and his oldest daughter's belt who was sitting in the front. His efforts were fruitless.

He shares that it felt like a giant hand grabbed him and pulled him with lightning speed to the surface. This is when he realized that the life of his three precious little girls came to an end!

A few minutes earlier, Michelle, drenched in gasoline in the icy waters, had unfastened her seatbelt. She also explains that it was as if she was pulled by some invisible hand up and out of the plane. She climbed onto the ice and was horrorstricken at what had just happened. She was numb with grief, shock, and disbelief and she thought she was the only survivor.

She stood beside that big hole in the ice assuming she'd lost not just her three daughters, but her husband as well. Then Jeremy burst from the surface of the frigid waters. Michelle had nothing left in her to help him as he struggled to pull himself onto the ice. She said it was a very "out of body" feeling, like watching something horrible happen and not being able to respond.

In the horrible moments to follow the plane crash, they found themselves embracing by the big hole in the ice and saying goodbye to three of their six children.

As they looked for a safe route to shore, Jeremy fell in the water at least two more times where Michelle was able to help him.

They knew of a cabin a couple of miles down the lake. They began to walk across the frozen lake when hypothermia began to take hold of Jeremy. First tunnel vision and then near collapse. Michelle steadied him as they made their way to the cabin.

This story cut me to the bone like none I'd ever heard! With three kids of my own, I can't imagine the moment that Jeremy had to make the decision to cut his own belt and leave those girls behind for the sake of his three remaining boys.

I cried sitting at that breakfast table, right there in the presence of the waitress, the cook and God Himself. We left.

We slept in one of those girls' beds that night, a new baby at rest a floor above us. Noah (New hope) Jesse (God exists) is his name. Not a replacement by any means, but a symbol of a promise for sure: a promise of redemption, a promise of hope.

As I sat at that table listening to two men, passionate about their relationship with the Maker, sharing simple stories of how He is working deeply in them through the most difficult of circumstances, I changed. It was as if the very hand of God reached down, touched my chin and gently raised my head to gaze into His eyes instead of toward my own situation. The tight grip of grief that had its selfish fingers wrapped tightly around my throat choking the life out of me began to loosen. For the first time in months, I felt like I could breathe again. As in the days of Adam; the Maker once again breathed His breath of life into a pile of dry dusty dirt. I felt free and alive—I began to look again toward the wide-open spaces and my soul awoke from his slumber.

My spirit was so happy to see the rest of me coming back to life—he was tired: tired of having to carry the load. He was exhausted from having to pick up one heavy foot and put it in front of the other over and over again, all by himself. I am thankful for my spirit's ability to make decisions and take action, for when the mind and emotion fail, he keeps things moving forward. But when all three can work together, the work happens almost effortlessly. Make no mistake, they cannot accomplish this task on their own, it requires the leadership of the Spirit of the Maker, for when the eyes of the three are on themselves or looking in different directions, they work against one another. But when they all look to the Redeemer and listen for the Spirit, the unity of the three accomplish the impossible.

And that is what I experienced that morning at the breakfast table. My body, soul and spirit began to work together and the three shifted their attention once again to the mission of the Maker. Like a team of sled dogs taking the life-saving meds to the isolated village to save the life of a wounded warrior, they began to forget about the hard work that lie ahead and began to enjoy the ride for what it was, a mutual mission to bring life to the lifeless and hope to the hopeless.

Redemption is a sweet thing!

My First Encounter with the Heroes

"In thinking back on the days of Easy Company, I'm treasuring my remark to a grandson, who asked, 'Grandpa, were you a hero in the war?'
'No,' I answered, 'but I served in a company of heroes.'"
- Mike Ranney from Stephen Ambrose's <u>Band of Brothers</u>[12]

We were scheduled to catch a plane from Anchorage to Port Alsworth. Merrill Field is a small airport dedicated mostly to small private planes. This little hub of activity always ranks within the top one hundred busiest airports in the U.S. It was certainly not because of its size, but its volume. After rolling through a locked gate, we strolled into the small, shared office area of Lake and Penn Air and Spernak Airways. Peter chatted with a couple of folks and I grabbed a cool cup of stale coffee.

The office reminded me of a place you would get your tires changed on your car and then complain about how much it costs. I overheard Peter talking to a young man that I would later know as Lyle. Lyle finished up with Peter and then made his way over to me. "Hey, I'm Lyle, there's a little problem with our plane. We're going to try to get it fixed."

This is when I learned for the first time that the key to surviving in Alaska is flexibility. I am like most other folks, I like to maintain control. When you are dealing with unpredictable weather, air travel and Alaska, you just have to hope for the best and hold on.

Turns out, the plane could not be repaired until some parts arrived the following day. Peter regrouped and decided that he would fly with another company and that I would take my first journey through Lake Clark pass with Nate. "Sure," I said. After all, what else could I do? I certainly couldn't fly myself over to Port Alsworth. So we hung around and waited for Nate to arrive. My next rescue vehicle would be a small two-seater bush plane, which would take me on the flight of a lifetime!

When Nate arrived, the three of us stopped at Subway and grabbed lunch. This would prove to be a big mistake as the day progressed. I am not one to get motion sickness, but then again I have never flown in a small bush plane through Lake Clark Pass while diving low to get good shots of wildlife through the lens of my Nikon.

On Our Way to Paradise

Nate and I made the short trip to Ted Stevens Airport, Anchorage's main hub and the home to Nate's small rescue boat. Nate made some last minute inspections and then in the cab we climbed for our two and a half hour-flight to Port Alsworth. As we flew over the Cooke Inlet, I enjoyed the views of the salmon fisheries and small rivers winding through the marsh as if they were lost in a corn maze. I noticed I was a little short of breath so I opened the air vent cut into the window at my two o'clock position. I wondered if I would make it all the way or if my claustrophobia would win the battle in this little plane where I was shoulder to shoulder with my only hope for a safe journey. Claustrophobia or not, there was nowhere to turn for relief; I would just have to stick it out and breathe deeply.

We saw a few moose as we were passing just outside of Anchorage; although they looked about the size of a large dog from fifteen hundred feet, I knew better. As the landscape began to change I saw my first black bear running in one of the winding rivers. Nate took me low for a closer view and I tried to shoot a few frames from the window of the plane, but the movement of the bear and the plane just gave me a blurry fuzz ball on my image screen. Although the images were not much to look at, the sight was breathtaking to the unaided eye! He looked up at us and ran through the water splashing and waving his head as he ran, almost as if he were a playful puppy with his faithful master. I would have never imagined something so beautiful.

This is what the heart of a man longs for in Alaska; this is why you only have to mention the word to get a man's blood pumping. We long for wilderness; we long for freedom. We have created a safety net with our nice homes in gated communities. We pull our safety rated car into our enclosed attached garages and push the button of our little electronic door closer. Life is safe. But the Maker did not intend for us to lock ourselves down in safe little gated communities. He placed deep in our heart a longing for adventure…to fight a battle.

Man was created in a garden! Our first task was to name the wild animals and bring order to the chaos into which we were placed. There is meaning and purpose in taming the wild. We are born to be on the front lines to do battle against the enemy. And we have chosen to live our lives avoiding the one thing that gives us meaning and purpose.

Matthew 11:12 has been interpreted in many ways, "From the days of John the Baptist until now the kingdom of heaven suffers violence, and violent men take it by force." Some say the forceful men are the persecutors of the Church while others say they are those zealous followers of Christ who lay hold of the Kingdom and claim it as a prize. Either way, force is involved. There is battle and danger and hard work, yet we have worked so hard to minimize the battle.

That bear running wild and free splashing through the rushing waters awakened something in my soul once again: a desire to passionately pursue my relationship with the Maker of it all. John Eldredge said, "A man's calling is written on his true heart, and he discovers it when he enters the frontier of his deep desires,"[13] and one of his deepest desire is to live and die for a purpose.

Three or four bears later and a couple of moose, we were passing over a glacier eerily resembling a freeway cut through the side of the mountain. Nate looked below and said with excitement, "Wow, I've got to get you down to see that monster bull."

I looked down and scanned the forest below and my eye caught him. He was massive! He stood with his head rocking back and forth under a rack that I could only imagine seeing late at night on one of those Discovery Channel shows. Nate rolled the plane around and headed for the ground with me making every effort to find him in my viewfinder and get one decent shot of this beautiful creature. I almost had him in my sights a couple of times as I zoomed in close to get a shot from four hundred feet up. He zigzagged in and out of my viewfinder. Just as I was giving up on a clean shot, I took my eye from the viewfinder and Nate made a quick upward turn to climb back to our cruising altitude. As he did, I had the unfortunate opportunity to revisit my Subway lunch as we met face to face for a second time.

Almost as if in slow motion, I had enough advance notice to turn my head away from Nate as my nose hit the glass of the window that almost wrapped around me. Lunch hit the window with a bang! It was everywhere. I felt so bad for Nate. There is no worse way to offend a bush pilot than to barf in his rescue boat. I was humiliated. If I was not already intimidated by my arrival at Port Alsworth and my first introduction to new friends that I would see for years to come, I was then. My first twenty minutes in paradise was spent with a sponge and some dish soap cleaning out the cab of a small bush plane. The next few minutes…borrowing a total stranger's washing machine to erase the evidence of my humiliating first experience in the bush of Alaska.

Although I felt terribly insecure at that point, it doesn't take barfing in someone's vehicle to make me insecure. I often wonder why I get so antsy around new folks and in new situations. I often try to convince myself that every person is alike; some are gifted in one area, while others are gifted in another. There is no reason for me to feel intimidated with new people, but I am a people pleaser and I have battled APPS since I was a child. New people mean new opportunities to make a bad first impression.

The fear of saying something stupid or doing something wrong often paralyzes me. I wonder if I will ever feel free to run in the wide-open spaces of new experiences without feeling trapped. When will I learn to be confident in the identity that the Maker has given me, instead of feeling incompetent trying to be a hero to everyone?

I had no problem trying to be the hero sitting in a pile of barf as we hit the runway at PA. Who could be a hero sitting in a pile of their own lunch?

The Maker has quite the sense of humor.

The Loving Arms of a Broken Family

As we made our descent upon the gravel runway, I could see a lady standing on the sidelines waving her hands through the air. Nate looked over and said, "There's my wife, it's good to see her." We taxied and pulled into the yard of the cabin owned by Uncle John; you remember the proverbial *John Wayne*? I had landed in paradise, I was sure. The small town of about a hundred and twenty in the summertime was more beautiful than anything I'd ever seen! The vegetation was so green, the people so alive, the community so supportive—I thought these places only existed on television. It was as if I stepped back one hundred years in history.

Peter felt we needed to survey the land where he would be leading our team on this wilderness adventure. Nate took both of us up and we flew over our intended route. To this day, I do not know why I agreed to take that flight after what had just happened a couple hours earlier, but I could not bear to miss seeing a sneak peak at what we would experience in the days to come.

When we returned, Peter and I spent a couple of hours preparing gear and food for the journey ahead and then made our way into the home of Jeremy and Michelle Davis, the parents of the sweet girls who died that wretched day on the lake.

Peter could not wait to get to the kitchen and pop open a jar of canned salmon and break out the Pilot Bread for a snack that took him back to memories of his

134

boyhood in Port Alsworth. After we laundered our clothes and had a snack, we got ready to bed down for the night. I was so excited I could hardly sleep in anticipation of what lie ahead my first full day in the bush.

As Peter showed me to our room for the night, I noticed it once belonged to children. Tears welled up in my eyes. I realized that the very beds we were about to sleep in were the ones those little girls, who died in that cold, deep lake, slept in for their few short years on Earth. The bathroom where we brushed our teeth had been the place where those cute girls learned to do the same just a few years before. How could a house once filled with such life be a place of refuge for a family who lost three angels on the same tragic day? How could a mother and father continue after such a nightmare come true?

Although I had briefly met Michelle a couple hours earlier, I was anxious to get to know this family who had suffered such tragedy. What must life be like now?

The next morning, Peter and I arose early and prepared for our day. I was feeling a keen sense of loneliness and homesickness as I began to realize that I would not be able to communicate with my wife and three little ones for about a week. I sat and thought about each of them. I pulled out the little picture I had tucked away in my backpack and imagined my little boy bursting into my bedroom early that morning to announce his arrival, anticipating how excited we would be to see him—he did that every morning for about a year. I imagined my little girl wrapping her arms around Daddy and saying in her little girl voice, "Daddy, come home now, we miss you."

135

The story I heard earlier that morning made the longing in my heart to be with them almost more intense than I could bear.

Later, Michelle called us in to breakfast and I got my first glimpse into the lives of these heroes. Jeremy looked at Michelle with a longing in his eyes, as if it was the best part of his day. Michelle seemed to anticipate Jeremy's arrival and you could tell how important it was for her to have everything ready. It only took a few minutes for me to realize their love for one another: a few more to realize their love for everyone who stepped inside the walls of their cozy Alaskan lodge.

The Davis family is a picture of the grace of the Maker. Like the rest of us, they aren't perfect, but they thrive to live their lives under the care of the Maker. It was as if this little broken family of six wrapped their loving arms around me, a weary, lonely traveler and patted me on the back to say, we are so glad you came. The homesickness I felt for my home felt lighter in the presence of this amazing family, who was a simple picture of the love of the Maker. What struck me most about the Davis' was how much they seemed to appreciate the gift of each other, of a new day of life and of whatever visitor found refuge in their cabin by the lake.

After breakfast I sat on the sofa in front of the triple window overlooking the spectacular shores of Lake Clark and the snow-capped mountain on the other side. I looked at a basket of books and picked up a photo album. As I began to thumb through, I realized it was a compilation of letters from around the country sent to console the Davis' in their loss. Some were handwritten while others printed in black and white. As I read the heartfelt words, I began to weep. I was thankful everyone had gone out to start their morning chores, for this could have been yet another humiliating experience with my new friends.

I began to realize that it was not just this mother and father who had lost three daughters, but across the country folks had lost nieces, cousins, friends, grandchildren, great-grandchildren, and sisters in Christ. I could not stop thinking about my little ones, ages five, two and just a few months. How could I ever endure such agony of knowing they were gone? There is only one explanation: it is only by the power of the Spirit of the Maker that I could pick one foot up and place it in front of the other time and time again until He led me to the edge of the River to drink of the water of redemption.

The Maker is a master at taking the worst tragedies of life and redeeming them into beautiful lenses through which we can look and see His beauty, His grace and His healing.

And there I slept in the bed of those girls, who no longer try to survive with the cheap imitations of the Love of God, but rest in the true peace of eternity at home with Redeemer. I suspect that to be the only thing that helped those parents get through life after the girls, knowing that they were safe and sound in His arms. A few years before, I would have snickered at that cliché, but that night I understood that the more tragedy we see, the more we long for what will come.

May we learn from Jeremy and Michelle what it looks like to fall headlong into the redemption and love of the Maker and His gift, Redeemer, and relinquish all control and expectation to Him in return for the abundant life He promises deep in the pages of His *Compass*.

There is a comfort beyond all logic, as we trust Him with every ounce of our lives and the lives of those around us. We must lay our head in His lap and call Him "Daddy," for it is Daddy who bears all the struggles and worries of this life in His hand, and allows us the opportunity to just be His children.

I have learned countless truths from spending time with the Davis'. The most poignant is to thank the Maker for every minute that He gives you with your loved ones. It is only after experiencing the absence of the girls that they could fully appreciate the presence of the boys. That appreciation for life spilled right out of them and into those around them.

It is common in Alaska for visitors to get a new sense of appreciation for what they have back home. Life is so fragile. Our manufactured comfort zones, in our safety net of civilization, have caused us to disregard this gift. We do not understand the value of the now, having protected ourselves from the danger and losses of yesterday. I am certainly not saying we are wrong in that; it is a privilege to not have to worry about that level of danger. However, we should find a way to remind ourselves that we are dispensable; that we are absolutely not in control. That, as Peter likes to say, "We are a grain of sand on the seashore, here today and gone tomorrow."

And when we are gone the world moves on. The Maker uses other Pilgrims on other journeys. Rich Mullins once said, "It's not a special thing to be used by God, for He uses anyone who opens their lives to Him and follows His lead. And He often even chooses to use folks that are not necessarily good people to get His will accomplished."

No, we are not the special ones for following: He is the special One for leading.

In my stubbornness, I often battle with a simple truth. Many stories do not end happily, there are often situations in life that cannot be explained, and the closest followers of Redeemer often doubt the Goodness of the Maker following unexplainable tragedies. But it is also true that the Maker loves His children and will never load them with burdens and weight too heavy to bear. He is the redeemer of all tragedy. He is the only One who can take life's most difficult struggles and use them to bring light and life to the darkness of another.

The Maker may be dangerous, He may be unpredictable, He may be unexplainable at times, but He loves His children. As singer/songwriter Jason Gray recently wrote in light of this, "Everything Sad is Coming Untrue." That's how this first encounter with the heroes helped me get past my own tragedy. No matter how bad our circumstances seem, He has led others through more difficult journeys. A fresh understanding of that can bring healing to our souls.

The First Hours in the Wilderness

Halfway through the day, Peter and I hopped in a motorboat and headed for our drop-off at the opposite shore of Lake Clark. We climbed out of the aluminum boat about five miles from where we climbed on. The ride across Lake Clark was spectacular with crystal clear skies and snow-capped mountains. The air was crisp and clean and the landscape was rugged. I was hoping I wouldn't wake to find it all just a dream. Our hair was waving to the opposite shore as we cut through the waves of that big lake. As we hopped off the boat and onto dry land, we hauled our gear to shore and waved goodbye to Nate as he pulled away and headed home. We would see Nate again in just a couple of days when he dropped off the remainder of our team, but for now, it was just Peter and me. There was a sense of loneliness like I felt when my college sweetheart departed for her summer internship. It was terrible, yet hopeful as I basked in the anticipation of what would come.

We would meet the other four guys two days later at this same spot. In the meantime, we planned to find the best route to our base camp about four miles in. Peter explained that we should arrive there by mid-afternoon and then we would hike back out and grab the rest of the gear. We hoisted the food bag up a tree so the wildlife would not be able to feast on our provisions.

On that first trip in, Peter packed about seventy-five pounds of camp gear and I was packing about forty-five. We pulled our packs to our back, buckled up and took off on my first journey into the Alaskan wilderness.

An hour in, we realized that something didn't seem right. We had expected to hit the banks of the Kijik River by that point. Peter realized that we had veered off course and that we would have to either backtrack or cut east to get to the river's edge. We cut east. It should have been an easy trek to the Kijik had it not been for some local beavers who decided to build a massive swamp in our path. As I contemplated whether to return as we had come or try to make our way through the swamp, Peter had already chosen the latter. He was knee deep in water and it looked as though we would go deeper. After a few more minutes, Peter said, "Take your pack off and hold it above your head at arms length." This was the first time on the trip that I wondered if this was what I had signed up for.

Ankle deep...knee deep...hip deep...chest deep. I began to wonder if Peter had lost his mind for leading me into this or if I had lost mine for following—maybe it was a little of both. There is really no danger in Alaska with water animals, as long as you don't drink from the water in which they relieve themselves. In Alabama we would surely have met at least a couple of water moccasins. In Alaska there are no snakes, no gators or anything else really to worry about as long as you don't spook a bear or moose. So we just waded.

After a few close calls with deep spots, we found ourselves looking over the edge of the Kijik. I was relieved to be out of the swampland. At this point, two hours later, we were where we should have been forty-five minutes into our trip. The next couple of hours were absolutely out of this world. Along one horizon were the deep turquoise waters of Lake Clark, while resting upon the other were the jagged peaks of Alaskan mountains. Occasionally, I would stop and snap off one of the bright purple flowers of the fireweed and marvel at its color and design. It hit me that I was a couple hundred miles from civilization and it was as if I was living a dream.

We walked along the Kijik stopping every so often to take a look at signs of life: prints, scat and rubbings. The bear prints were amazing: the size of them hard to believe. The scat, post-digestion remnants of last night's meal, was fresh and that made me more than a little nervous. I had imagined what it must be like to roam that close to such beasts, but it was not reality until I saw the proof that they were walking with me. It made me feel both vulnerable and miniscule.

The sun began to drop lower and lower and we had failed to reach our destination. The terrain got tougher. We were side-stepping a huge mountain and my ankles were beginning to give. When I thought we must be arriving at camp, we just kept crossing one foot over the other traversing the side of the mountain. After another hour or so it took every ounce of energy I could muster to pick one foot up and try to lift it over the other. Focus, step, focus, step: the concentration it took just to take that next step was exhausting. Peter was struggling too—I could see it in his movements. It became evident that we had misjudged our capabilities or underestimated the length of the journey. We had packed one pouch of dehydrated food each and I was beginning to sweat. What if we didn't make it back tomorrow? What would we eat?

It is never really as bad as it feels when you face challenges such as this, but your mind plays nasty games on you and you imagine the worst. My mind was making some noise. Pop...my ankle had turned. The pain began to deepen; the throbbing pulsed. I felt like I could not move another inch. As I was struggling to pick my left foot up and swing it over my right, Peter yelled. I looked up and he had dropped to the ground and was gripping his legs in pain. We had not drunk enough water and had not eaten in a few hours. Peter's legs tightened with severe cramps.

He was determined to move on.

"If we could just get to the other side of the river the terrain would be easier," he said. "I'm going to try to cross here."

I looked into the crystal clear water and it looked to be deeper than either of us. The current was relatively calm, but in Alaska even that can take you swimming down the river in forty-degree waters. Peter stripped off every stitch of clothing, put everything he was carrying over his shoulders and stepped in. "Come on."

"I'm not going," I said. "If you make it, I'll think about it, but I'm not going yet."

"Okay," he said as he stepped into the stream. The cold took his breath away. I watched him take his first few steps and then sink to neck deep waters. His feet started bobbing up and down. He was beginning to be swept away! "I'm slipping, I'm slipping. Pray for me, Kevin!"

I watched helplessly as Peter lost his footing. I wanted to help, but how? What should I do? He floated one hundred feet downstream and every connection to the outside world was on his shoulders: satellite phone, two-way radios, everything. As I watched, my mind began to work very quickly, but in slow motion. You know how that feels—like every second is an hour and you have all the time you need to imagine the worst and hope for the best. I thought about my wife and kids. I imagined what it would be like to not return home. All the while watching and thinking about how I could help. I was a rookie in the bush, so I did what most ignorant rookies do; I watched.

I looked downstream and saw Peter struggling against the current. Somehow he made his way back to shore with the pack still above his head. As I stood there, I was sure the Maker stood with us. I think had He not been, Peter would have been taken by the current and I would have been trapped alone in the dark in a place much bigger than I could handle. As much as I hate to admit it, I couldn't think about much but myself. I had experienced my first brush with danger in the wilderness of Alaska.

We made a wise decision, albeit a little late, to bed down for the night and pick up where we left off the following morning. We shared one pack of dehydrated food and fell fast asleep in utter exhaustion. I wondered where our next meal would come from.

My mind is a trickster! It manipulates most things. It is amazing how circumstances seem to change depending on my mood. The years following this trip seemed much less challenging than the first. When you accomplish a feat once, it seems half as difficult the next time. There is a new standard of difficult and if we ever get beyond it, it seems everything before is a breeze. I have learned to control the raging monster in my mind during difficulties in which I am out of control. Sometimes you just keep moving. Your thoughts will follow. It works the same with faith. The Maker speaks, the wild Stallion in our mind rears up on two feet in protest, he comes to his senses and breathes deeply, calms himself and you move on, one step in front of the other as the Spirit gives direction and *The Compass* shows the way. For it is the Spirit that is ultimately the path to more than you could otherwise accomplish. Maybe that is what happened to Peter in the river that day. Logic says no, Spirit says yes. His mind was his limitation; his will was his hero. When we listen to the voice of the Maker compelling us to follow and things seem to be impossible, just wake up the Spirit within and let Him speak.

Follow.

Submit.

Walk by faith and you'll find your way.

Peter Ready to Meet a Bear

Our Place

"The world is round and the place which may seem like the end may also be only the beginning." - Ivy Baker Priest.

"What lies behind us and what lies before us are tiny matters compared to what lies within us." - Henry Stanley Haskins

"You're blessed when you're at the end of your rope. With less of you there is more of God and His rule." Jesus, *The Compass*, Matthew 5:3, MSG

I cannot take any more of this!

Have you ever come to the end of yourself? Have you ever felt like your next step would be the one that sent you high flying off the edge of a cliff?

There I was, emotionally and physically looking over the edge. I wanted to go home so badly. I wanted to return to my family, the ones who embraced me just as I was. I wanted to wrestle with my kids because they think I am superhuman. I wanted to hug my wife because she knows me and loves me still. The problem was that I could not run away because I was stuck; I could not choose to walk away from this adventure because I didn't have a bush plane. If I would have had a plane, I wouldn't be able to fly it. And if I could have flown it, I wouldn't have known my way out of this crazy place. I think the Maker had me stuck there so I would have to fight my way out of this anger inside of me...this frustration that was caused by me being out of control. The familiar foe of insecurity led me to the edge of that cliff and I was on the verge of stepping right into his trap once again.

We never made it to our base camp. We spent a day or so recovering from the physical exertion and caught a few fish to feed us until we returned back and picked up the remainder of our group. We trekked for two days into the campsite we would call home for the next three. I did not enjoy those couple days with our new friends, mostly due to the familiar foe in this uncomfortable place with new people. Insecurity has been a theme in my life from what seems like the beginning—it was the monkey always riding on my back.

When I was a boy, I was far from athletic. I tried to play basketball in first and second grade. At that young age it was obvious that I didn't have a career ahead of me on the court. I remember as a seven-year-old boy feeling watched...feeling laughed at. One of my earliest memories of basketball was getting my first jersey. I am quite sure the coach felt sorry for me. He seemed to be my cheerleader, prodding me onward from the sidelines. But the more I tried, the more I made a fool of myself. I had no clue what I was doing. When we were picking jersey numbers he said, "What number you want to be, son?" I never thought about having a number, so I looked at him with a blank stare. He looked back with compassion and said, "What about seven? Seven is a good number. It's God's favorite number. Yeah, seven...God will be with you."

I don't know why this coach chose seven; maybe he felt sorry for me and hoped God would redeem my basketball skills. Then again maybe he didn't choose it at all; maybe the Maker chose that number. Maybe even at the age of eight, He was tapping me on the shoulder saying, "Hey kid, it's not about your basketball skills, it's about wearing my number. You can do it. Wear my number."

The first time I had a chance to take the court wearing the blue, sacred number seven on the front of my gray t-shirt which doubled as a uniform, I miraculously rebounded a wild shot by my teammate and headed as fast as I could dribble, which was not very fast, straight for the wrong goal. I heard the crowd screaming. What an amazing experience for a young boy! Destiny was in my hands in the form of an orange ball and I was running as fast as I could in the wrong direction. I felt like an officer in the infantry leading his team into a battle they were sure would be the final victory of a hard fought war. I made it across enemy lines, launched the ball airward, and watched. As if in slow motion, it hit the rim and bounced off heading into the abyss of what I thought to be defeat. The crowd went wild!

Why are they so excited about me missing the shot? I wondered. Later, I would find out. Not only had I shot at the wrong goal; I missed, and so somehow I won that game for my team. The courage I felt as I dribbled that ball down the court turned into a nagging fear of failure that would follow me straight into the Alaskan bush that day in early August, twenty-seven years later.

Why the Maker would want such a basketball flunky to wear his number I will never know. Maybe He delights in the flunkies. Maybe it is through the weak things of this world that His beauty and perfection are made known. Redemption is a beautiful thing! What appears to be failure and humiliation to us is simply an opportunity for the Maker to be lifted up. I am so thankful for number seven.

Paul wrote most of the New Testament; wouldn't you think he'd be just about perfect? He had something to say about this weakness and strength business when he wrote to a church in this big city called Corinth:

"Because of the extravagance of those revelations, and so I wouldn't get a big head, I was given the gift of a handicap to keep me in constant touch with my limitations. Satan's angel did his best to get me down; what he in fact did was push me to my knees. No danger then of walking around high and mighty! At first I didn't think of it as a gift, and begged God to remove it. Three times I did that, and then he told me, "My grace is enough; it's all you need. My strength comes into its own in your weakness." *The Compass,* 2 Corinthians 12:7-10.

Once I heard that, I was glad to let it happen. I quit focusing on the handicap and began appreciating the gift. It was a case of Christ's strength moving in on my weakness. Now I take limitations in stride, and with good cheer, these limitations that cut me down to size— abuse, accidents, opposition, bad breaks. I just let Christ take over! And so the weaker I get, the stronger I become.

The morning that we picked up the other guys I had a number seven experience.

Mike was a man's man. As soon as we picked him up by the side of the lake, he began to share his story of running the Iron Man Triathlon in Hawaii a few years back. He was confident that although he was the oldest on the trek at sixty, he would have no trouble with the physical demands it would present. Mike was the kind of guy that knocked on the door of my familiar foe and invited him to come out and play. The familiar foe joyfully accepted the invitation and there I was in the middle of the basketball court all over again.

I was determined that it would be different this time. I would not run toward the opposing goal, but would keep my composure, stay cool and hang with the best of these guys. As we were about to cross a small branch of the river, Mike asked, "What do you do for a living?"

Never had I been more compelled to tell a blatant lie! "Well, I lead a ministry in Auburn."

"So you're a pastor," he bellowed. "Hey guys, we've got a preacher with us."

My greatest nightmare had come true! "Now you're in trouble," said the friendly foe of insecurity.

Five minutes later, it was time to cross the river. I stepped in with confidence. I had been out here for two days and I was sure I could handle this little challenge. Each step took me a few inches deeper into the river. When I was waist deep, my foot dropped onto a slippery rock and I fell right into the hands of the friendly foe once again. Mike grabbed me and firmly lifted me off my butt and pushed me to the opposite side of the river. My identity shifted from the assistant guide who had his act together to the preacher who would be the weak link on this trek for real men. Once again, I was wearing my number seven! My greatest fear for this trek in the bush had come true. How would I recover? I spent the remainder of that day rolling around in the feces of self-pity.

The following day, I breathed out a sigh of relief as the attention shifted from me to Mark. The second day of this trek included a difficult trip over the shoulder of a mountain. I made it a couple days earlier, so the second time over seemed effortless. As I mentioned, physical challenges are always easier the second time. It is not as much about how physically fit as it is about how mentally tough we are. It is the unknown that defeats us mentally. When we do not know what the next step holds, our feet have a harder time taking it. That second trip over the ridge was a breeze.

The other guys were struggling...particularly Mark. He was stopping every five minutes asking for a break. I felt so bad for him, for I remembered a similar experience on Lazy Mountain. Ironically, at the same time, I felt a sense of relief that it was not I. He was hurting! About halfway up the mountain, Peter instructed me to move on with the three other guys while he stayed behind to help his dad. And there I was; the weak pastor with lucky number seven metaphorically plastered across my back, ironically leading the tri-athlete and his cohorts. I felt some sense of redemption course through my veins as off we went.

On the other side of the mountain two hours later, we waited. A sense of concern rushed through my mind as we waited some more. An hour later we heard some guys talking straight up the mountain behind us. Another fifteen minutes and we caught our first glimpse of the other two making their way down. As they got closer, we realized that Mark did not have a pack on his back. I wondered who would go back up the mountain to retrieve it. Then I saw Peter. He had his seventy-five-pound pack on his back and Mark's fifty-pound pack draped over his chest. The rest of us could barely make it up and down that mountain with one pack; Peter carried two.

As they cut their way through the undergrowth and the full story of what had happened became clear, I began to weep. What a beautiful picture of family. Mark was a good father who loved his son with a love only a father could feel. But, like all fathers, he had made mistakes. And Peter was a rebel at heart who must have been a raging bull as a boy. In Alaska we often end up, at some point during the trip, talking about father

154

wounds. We never have an agenda for this, but when you put a guy in the wilderness for a week and take him out of the distractions of life, these types of things are what he usually thinks about. He usually begins to dream again and when we dream about a better future, we think about why we are not living the life the Maker meant for us to live. Father wounds are the moments when the most impactful man in a boy's life speaks mediocrity or, even worse, defeat into his heart. Father wounds are like little seeds that get lodged into a boy's heart and grow into vines that choke him of the fullness of what he could have been...what he was born to do and be.

Every father/son relationship has some measure of brokenness and pain through father wounds. Peter is a man of passion and as long as Mark can remember, Peter has had a warrior spirit. Peter tells of a day when they were sitting in the parking lot of a department store and just across the road was a manufacturing plant. Peter was a young boy and was dreaming about his future. He looked over and asked his dad what he thought Peter would do when he grows up. Mark looked at him with every good intention and said, "Well, Peter, I think you'll be a great supervisor at a manufacturing plant like that one over there."

"*A manufacturing plant?*" Peter thought. How could the most important man in his life, the one who speaks identity into his heart and propels him into manhood and adventure think of him as a supervisor at a manufacturing plant? Peter dreamed of hunting bears and fighting battles; exploring the universe and saving lives. A supervisor?

Some of us respond to father wounds by living into them; Peter spent the rest of his young-adulthood fighting with every ounce of his being to be more than just a supervisor at a manufacturing plant. That's what drove Peter to do the very things that most men can only dream of. Peter was fearless in that pursuit. Whether he was riding a bull or tackling a stretch of white water most men would shy away from, scaling a mountain peak or tracking a brown bear, Peter was willing to die for his passion as opposed to the alternative.

There I stood, watching the most beautiful picture of redemption a man could witness: the wounded carrying the weight of the *wounder*. But not out of rebellion, out of love. If Peter had been acting in rebellion, he would have taken an attitude...*you carry your own damn pack...or die. I don't care.* And Mark would have felt a sense of defeat and rejection. It was not that at all. Peter had true compassion for his father and was willing to sacrifice for his sake. Mark had a sense of pride well up in him like a dad must have felt watching his son drag half-dead people out of the rubble of 9/11.

As the four of us stood and watched those two walking nearer, laughing and smiling from ear to ear, a new sense of camaraderie wedged its way into that group at the bottom of the mountain. How could Peter do this? How could a man get his mind off himself in this kind of challenge in order to carry the load of another? Could I have made that same commitment? Was it just because it was Peter's dad, or would he have done this for me too? My perspective changed at that moment. My arrogant pride of leading these men over that mountain, turned into the humility of knowing that, presented with Peter's dilemma, I could not have carried the load of another man. And if I had had the physical ability to do so, I would not have had the emotional commitment to follow through.

These events led me straight to the edge of the cliff. The partnership of emotional and physical challenges, as we made our way to base camp left me at the end of myself. I felt as though the experiences that lie ahead were not worth the cost of getting there and I wanted to hang it all up. In addition to those challenges, I had faced unmet expectations from the three other guys that made me want to part ways and move on to other relationships with other men who were more like me. I had hoped that these men would have the same level of pride and arrogance as I in being here to "find God." I had hoped that I would be able to take this journey with others who felt like they had the power to conjure up some super spiritual experience in the wilderness. Instead, I found myself with a group of men who I perceived were just there to experience the wilderness of Alaska. Couple that with the selfishness of the grief of my past year and you get a bastard child; one not walking in the image of his father, the Maker, but created by an illegitimate relationship between the enemy of his soul and the wounds of life, especially the wounds of the preceding year.

We finally arrived at that temporary three-day resting place. Peter bellowed out, "Here we are guys. Our home away from home."

I dropped my pack, stormed over to Peter and said, "Man, I gotta get alone for a little while."

Peter saw the anger in me. Later, I would find out he was doing battle with his own bastard child. I was too selfish to see it at the time. Off I went for a spontaneous unexpected meeting with the Maker.

Our Place

"But who can duly adore that Love which will open the high gates to a prodigal who is brought in kicking, struggling, resentful, and darting his eyes in every direction for a chance

157

of escape? The words 'compelle intrare' compel them to come in, have been so abused by wicked men that we shudder at them; but, properly understood, they plumb the depth of the Divine mercy. The hardness of God is kinder than the softness of men, and His compulsion is our liberation." - C.S. Lewis in Surprised by Joy[14]

I traveled about a hundred yards from camp. Those hundred yards seemed like one hundred miles. For the first time, I was alone in the wilderness of Alaska. I felt vulnerable and naked. As I passed by fresh bear poop and large areas carved out like crop circles where bear would fish and sleep, the fear of danger crept in to try to steal away what I would experience over the next couple hours. I contemplated a return to safety, but the level of need to be released from this anger and grief was greater than the level of fear, so I journeyed onward. I knew that I was at the precipice and wondered if I would have what it would take to lay hold of what lie ahead. The grass was shoulder height and its blades were an inch thick. The air smelled distinctly like a mix of fresh cut grass and ankle deep mud. Twenty hours of daylight and a plentiful water supply gave the vegetation what it needed to grow beyond what the limitations presented by average climates, just as the solitude and peace that I was about to find caused me to grow a few inches taller in my faith that morning; the vulnerability I felt was a passageway into that growth.

I walked until I felt done walking. I surveyed the area and found a spot right beside the lake to plop down and search for relief. As I hit the ground, I realized that I was hidden. I wondered if a bear or moose would stumble upon me and be startled enough to attack, but I didn't care. I sat. I thought. I decompressed. The anger in my soul burned hot. I was mad at Peter for bringing me here. I was mad at the Maker for letting me come. I wallowed in the dislike I had for the three others. My flesh was simmering over the hot flame of my lack of self-control—I waited.

How often does a person literally feel all the ugliness inside him rise to the surface and boil? I felt like I wanted to escape, but I had nowhere to run. I wanted to be somewhere else and I wanted to be someone else. My mind rolled around like the sea in that movie *The Perfect Storm*. I was out of control and I hated it. I asked for the Maker to rescue me and my head fell back in the tall grass. I lay there a helpless pile of flesh and bones with nowhere to go and hide from the monster that was doing battle against my soul.

As my eyes closed, the silence of the wilderness began to whisper in my ear. I sat for a few minutes and the whisper grew into a still small voice and I realized it was no longer the sound of the wilderness, but the sound of the Maker beckoning me to a better place. It took me by surprise and I listened more intently.

"Sit up and look."

I obeyed. When I arose from my slumber of defeat, I opened my eyes to a new life...a new perspective of the Maker.

I peered across the glassy lake to the other side where I saw three gorgeous mountain peaks. The vegetation at the bottom was lush and colorful and the rock faces got bluer as my eyes climbed to the top of the mountains. The reflection they produced in the still lake below took my breath away. It was the most beautiful site I had ever seen and through it the Lover was calling my name. "Kevin," He said, "no one has ever in the history of the universe sat right here in this spot and worshipped me. You are the first. I led you here to tell you that this is our place...yours and mine. I want you to know how loved you are. So much that I would pick this spot just for you."

I had truly stepped off the cliff and fallen headlong into the love of God! All the selfishness of the past days began to fall away. All the insecurities of the life of this broken little boy on the basketball court began to become secure in His love. My anger for those men turned into compassion and mercy. My frustration with the Maker melted away into appreciation for His love. I was changed. All the ugliness that was flooding out of me was washed away by a more forceful flood...the flood of His grace!

Over the next few minutes, our relationship changed. The person who had simply been the Maker of Creation became my Lover. The courtship became the proposal and I reluctantly and joyously accepted His offer. As far as I was concerned, this moment was the reason the Lover whispered into Scott's ear a few years ago as he met with the gypsies and said, "I'm going to Alaska and I think you are supposed to go with me." This proposal was not the first and it will not be the last, but it was an invitation to enter into the next level of this ever-growing relationship.

I lay my head down after this experience and peacefully drifted off to sleep. An hour or so later, I awoke and headed back to camp after one of the most peaceful naps of my life. I found Peter smiling from ear to ear. He shared a similar experience and we laughed and headed off to prepare the evening meal with joy in our hearts and compassion for the men that we had just hours ago wanted to send packing.

For the first time in the Alaskan bush, my soul was at rest.

God Wrote His Name

"Our Place" was a turning point for me on this first adventure in the Alaskan bush. It was like a before and after experience at a weight loss center. When we have a before and after experience our perspective changes. For example, when Mark had to submit to having his pack carried over the mountain, I felt better about myself. The ugly truth about pride and self-focus is that the only way it can be satisfied apart from a before and after experience is to glory in other people's failures or weaknesses. When someone else shows a greater weakness, my own rises up the ladder of the food chain—I only look good when others look bad. So I build an entire identity on others' failures. That is a miserable way to live…when my success depends on another's failures. But after my before and after experience, that story felt different. I could have compassion for my fellow travelers on this journey.

After I experienced that level of love and grace, I really think I could have carried Mark's pack right up that mountain and right back down. When we find a love that is beyond the love we have the capacity to show, it motivates us to share it, no matter the cost.

When I had first met Mike, I was still living in the before. I saw Mike through the eyes of my selfishness and arrogance. Mike took every opportunity he could to let us know he had run the Iron Man in Hawaii. It was his security blanket that made him feel safe in the midst of the unknown. Before the After, I had viewed Mike through the eyes of my own insecurity. Now I had changed—when I looked at him I saw a fellow traveler on this journey. I wanted to know him, to discover what made him tick and what it was that led him down this path of insecurity. I wanted to understand the things about Mike that have the capacity for greatness; what strengths had God given him to balance out those proverbial thorns in his flesh?

Mike viewed himself as a hero sent to rescue the lost soul. I am sure he had rescued a few stranded wanderers along the way too. One night we were sitting around the campfire just talking like guys do around campfires. I was tired of surface talk and I thought Mike was in a vulnerable place. So I popped out the question, "Mike, why do you think God's got you here?" I was expecting an answer that would drive conversation to a deeper level. Instead I got a response that caused me to shake my head and wonder if I would ever be able to have a reasonable conversation with this guy.

"Well, Kevin, I'm not sure which one of you I am here for. I'm just waiting to see."

I was speechless. Could that really be how he felt? Could any man ever assume that the Maker had brought him out to this place in this kind of solitude totally removed from life as he knew it…for someone else?

A couple of days later, we had found a canoe banked along the side of Kijik Lake and used it to get to the other side. There we found a beautiful sandy beach with a large open area to camp. It was a total change from our previous camp in the middle of the woods. We began to notice that Mike was breaking; he was quiet, reclusive and reflective. It was our fifth day in. Mike took Peter off away from the crowd and asked if he thought we could go in a day early so he and the boys could have a day in Anchorage to shop. Peter made up some lame excuse about not being able to get a flight out of Port Alsworth and went on with his day.

The next day, Peter and the two younger guys took a day hike up the mountain. I had twisted my ankle a day earlier so I stayed behind with Mark and Mike. One of

162

the three of us went down by the lake and lay on the sand for a few minutes of rest. The other two soon followed and we were lined up like seals beached for the afternoon.

I had a book in my hand when I looked up to the sky to think for a moment. As soon as my eyes rose to the deep blue background, I saw it. It was as clear as the handwriting in my journal! Right across the blue sky the clouds carefully converged to form the letters: *J.C.*

I was just about to say something to the other guys and Mike piped up with the voice of a little boy on Christmas morning. "Would you look at that?"

Mark and I both knew what he was talking about and we were both a little taken aback. I looked over at Mike and tears began to roll down his cheek. Maybe those were the first tears he had shed in years, who knows. He said as innocently as one could imagine, "God wrote his name in the sky for me."

And He did!

God took the time and effort to speak those clouds right into the shape of the letters *J.C.* I had never seen anything like it before and I have not since. We could not argue with the facts before our eyes. The Maker of the Universe scribbled His initials right above us like He scribbled on the ground the day He was standing with the religious freakos and the adulteress two thousand years earlier. And it was as if He were saying to Mike just as He did to the freakos..."You who are without sin cast the first stone. Now, go and sin no more."

Mike had his before and after experience right there on that sandy beach in front of Mark, me, and several thousand large, scary mosquitoes.

Mike was not the same after that experience. I never heard anything else about the Iron Man...when you see the power of the Maker of the Universe, the little things we do seem to drift away with yesterday's breeze.

You know, those clouds did not mean much to me. You could not argue that it was a dramatic moment, but my logical mind would have found a way to write the experience off as an amazing coincidence. But when I looked over to Mike and realized that his heart was penetrated with the piercing arrow of the love of God, what Brennen Manning calls a reckless raging fury, I knew that it was no stroke of luck. I had witnessed some form of miracle right before my eyes. That miracle penetrated right through that fallow ground of Mike's heart as if the plow had just been sharpened and the ground moistened with an early spring shower. I am thankful that I was able to be there the day Mike saw God write His name in the sky.

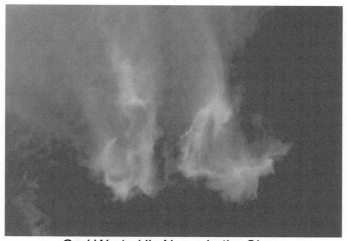

God Wrote His Name in the Sky

There's a wideness in God's mercy
I cannot find in my own
And He keeps His fire burning
To melt this heart of stone
Keeps me aching with a yearning
Keeps me glad to have been caught
In the reckless raging fury
That they call the love of God"
- Rich Mullins, "The Love of God"

There have been so many times when my faith would wane, the fourth quarter coming to a close and my team behind by fourteen. Sometimes life seems hopeless. The problems appear bigger than the solution; it is usually then that God writes His name right across the window of my life.

Just this week, my back was against a wall and the weight was pressing in and crushing the life right out of me. Just when I thought I was going to break, a small drop of hope literally fell from the sky. Then several drops fell. Then big drops; the kind you can feel hit the sidewalk in front of you. The kind that makes the metal of your car ring when it hits. *Ping.* Then the Maker just let those drops keep falling until I was saturated with His grace and peace. Thud.

Just one week ago, seven days, I was rolling around in the pit of hopelessness trying to fix my own problem out of desperation, feeling that God had turned His back to walk. Today I am writing this paragraph with a new assurance that He is still aware of my situation. He is still my Daddy as sure as He breathed His breath of life into man. I am still His son and He will not withhold His goodness and provision. He is able! So able that He may even choose to write His name in the sky to let me know that He still cares.

166

These sky-writing moments happen from time to time to get us back in His groove. We are wandering souls, bent on our own way. When He sees a need, He'll take out his figurative writing pen and craft the perfect story to get us back where He called us to be in the first place.

God, keep on writing.

Mark Brings Home Dinner

Rites of Passage and Family Ties

"What can you do to promote world peace? Go home and love your family." - Mother Theresa

The following year, in 2009, I was able to make the Original Design trip with one of the gypsies from the 1996 trip. It was so great to be able to be back "home" with the man who was responsible for introducing me to the last frontier. Scott had returned to Alaska several times since our 1996 trip, but this was the first time he was able to spend a week in the bush. I felt even more at home in the place where it all began as I journeyed with the person with whom it all began.

I flew into Anchorage a few days before the rest of the crew arrived. Peter and I spent the first couple of days together shopping for supplies and preparing for the outing. After a day or so in Anchorage, we loaded up with a family member of his and rode to Kenai to meet up with "Uncle John", previously referred to as *John Wayne*. As it turned out, Uncle John would take us over to Port Alsworth in his plane, a four-seater on floats. I had never landed on water, so I was excited about flying into Port Alsworth and floating into the shore of that beautiful bay.

As we were preparing to fly out, we sat down to an amazing plate full of Lasagna at the table of Uncle John. We listened as he and another Alaskan adventurer, Rocky McElveen, shared stories from the bush. As I listened to these men spout off their adventures, the little boy on the basketball court began to speak to my heart again. "You could never measure up to these real men," he said with his head bowed low. All of a sudden I am face to face, once again, with the insecurities of boyhood.

As we finished dinner and the McElveen family made their way back to the place from where they came, we gathered up our stuff and headed for Uncle John's plane beached in a lake not too far from where we were.

Peter let me ride in the front seat, hoping that I would not have another "Subway" episode like last year. I heartily concurred. I buckled up and we were off to Port Alsworth for our next adventure.

An hour or so into the trip I began to experience that all too familiar feeling of suffocation and nausea. No! I can't go through this humiliation again, especially not with *John Wayne*. I faintly heard Peter's voice through my headset, "If you get to feeling sick, just puke in your shirt or something, and whatever you do, take off your headset!" He passed forward over my shoulder an orange dry bag about the size of one of those white plastic bags you put in the trash can beside your toilet.

Five minutes later, I began to feel sick. It came on so fast and furious that I felt like I didn't have time to take off my headset and somehow (to this day I don't understand how) I missed the orange dry bag with all the force my abdomen could muster! It was everywhere.

Uncle John cried out, "What the hell are ya doin', boy?" Peter's voice came booming through the headset, "I told you to take your headset off!"

And there I sat, speechless, covered in lasagna wondering how God could turn His back on me at such an important time as this.

I sat quietly for a minute or two, which seemed like a hundred. The next thing I heard thundering through the cabin of the plane was, "God, that stinks." I wish it would have come from the back seat, at least I would have felt like I could have fought back when we reached the ground, but it didn't. It was Uncle John, the Alaskan legend, sitting at the seat of the plane that had taken him to the remotest parts of the Alaskan wilderness to shoot bears and catch wild fish, barking out the words that no one would want to hear two thousand feet in the air cramped up in a sardine can with nowhere to escape.

It was only by the grace of God that I didn't open that hatch and take a dive deep into the Alaskan wilderness, for that's what I wanted, and even desperately planned to do, as the humiliation lingered. It would have almost been easier to face the wild grizzlies and mad moose below than to look *John Wayne* in the eyes after what had just happened.

Then I realized the nightmare wasn't over as my abdomen began to convulse again. Yep. It happened. Fortunately, the humiliation of the earlier episode taught me a valuable lesson: in times such as this, never procrastinate! I quickly removed my headset, pretty much placed my head completely inside the orange dry bag and let 'er rip again. I wouldn't have dared miss this time.

As we were flying into the Lake Clark area, we made a quick descent into Kijik Lake to drop some gear at our campsite for the week. As we floated to a stop near the edge of the bank, I began to scoop up as much as my leftover lasagna as possible and throw it into the lake. Once again, floating right there in that lake beside the remnants of that humiliating experience, was every ounce of pride that was left in my pitiful personhood.

And whether I liked it or not, somehow, it was a source of healing for me. Somehow a second visit to the fountain of humiliation became my rite of passage into accepting the fact that I didn't measure up to the standards of the men of the wilderness. And in some strange way, that made me more of a man.

As we took off again and flew to the other side of the mountain and into the bay at Port Alsworth, the wind picked up and it was a rough landing in *John Wayne's* rescue boat. Uncle John was barking orders about what we would do when we came to a stop and how it was important for us to move quickly. I remember my mind whirling around thinking, does he want me to stay put or get out?

I had no clue what to do as Uncle John reached over me and threw open the exit hatch. It felt like everything was moving at warp speed. As I sat there paralyzed, he looked me in the face and said, "Whatchya doin', boy? Get out!"

I jumped out as quickly as possible, almost tripping over myself as I landed on the pontoon, and *John Wayne* fired up the engine, Peter hopped in a boat, and they both sped to the other side of the lake to dock the plane, leaving me all alone on the banks of the lake that rocked my world a year ago.

There I sat in thirty miles-per-hour wind hunkered down next to a little wooden cabin with rain stinging the side of my face...alone...empty...humiliated... wondering what the heck I was supposed to do next. I really don't want to tell you this, but it's true and I would probably be doing you some type of disservice to leave the detail out as much as I would like to. I began to cry. It's not something a man does that often, and

172

certainly not something I care to share with the world, but it's the honest-to-goodness truth. I cried.

I'm glad I was alone and I think I even vowed to never share the story with anyone. As a matter of fact, this is my third rewrite of these stories and I've finally found the courage to share it. But I think part of our problem as men is that we fail to tell each other we're vulnerable. We live our lives as our own gods and we think that somehow there is valor in that. We even work hard to give other men permission to be their own gods. The truth is, we are not God and God would love for us to know that. And so I tell you this part of the story so that you will know that it's okay to be human.

How you experience your humanity may look very different from this experience. It may look like moral failure, financial failure or a dead-end career, but it's okay. *The Compass* tells us that His power is made perfect in our weakness. We must realize that we are not gods, but that we come to know the God. And it is often times like this that we find our way out of the wilderness and into the promised land of manhood.

When you find yourself sitting on the banks of an experience such as this, with the wind and rain beating you down and you're all alone, remember that there is always hope on the other side. Time heals and it often doesn't move as quickly as we'd like. When it feels like all hell has broken loose and God has turned His back, that's when we often wake up the next morning and realize that we have found Him...at long last we've found Him.

And our hearts rejoice.

A Watery Rite of Passage

Another young man journeyed with us this year. Hailing from Nashville, Tennessee, Ben was taking his

173

first trip to Alaska. I was glad Ben was with us. I learned a lesson on tough love and rights of passage, and, like the rest of the travelers, Ben became more of a man.

As it is with most twenty-something men, Ben was facing a very difficult time in his life. In their mid-twenties men often realize that every major life decision is staring them in the face. Twenty-something-year-old men have wills of iron. They are still fighting for control of their lives. They don't want to let go of the girls, games and toys of boyhood. Things often haven't turned out exactly as they had expected and they have not yet become comfortable with being uncomfortable. Ben was experiencing all of this as he took his trek into the bush.

Mark served as a father figure for Ben during this trip, urging him to let go and let the Maker lead him to freedom. Ben was struggling in his heart with insecurity, fear and loneliness. Although he was dating an amazing girl, he still felt alone in this thing called life. He had tried a couple of business ventures and nothing seemed to be working. He was harboring an anger and restlessness that was getting the best of him.

Mark had walked through his share of these battles and he was determined to do what he could to help Ben dig his way through the tunnel.

During our weeklong trek, we often take a day to spend alone. We will pair up in groups of two and head in different directions—we try to stay in earshot of our partner, but we spend the time alone. Ben fought it like an angry wasp. His anger was probably a defense mechanism. When a man has been in the bush for a few days, he has nothing else to think about but the things that matter. All the fat burns away and he is left only with the meat. That's a scary thing for a man to deal with. He has worked so hard back home to medicate the deep pain that screams at him late at night. He has drowned it out with TV, sports, pornography, work or whatever else quiets the raging within. As the fat burned away, Ben fought hard, but in the end he submitted.

It was a gorgeous day, seventy degrees and blue skies. Mark paired up with Ben and we went our separate ways. As Ben and Mark were hiking a trail along the river, a storm cloud rolled in. And then the rain began. A huge rain!

Ben looked up as the rain began to pound to the ground. "Dammit! I can't believe this."

"What's wrong, Ben?"

"I left my tent open."

Ben turned to run back to camp, but Mark refused to let him go. "You can't go, Ben. You just have to face the consequences. I am out here and you're my partner. I'm not going. You have to be here."

Ben's anger flared and he was faced with one of those decisions that make you want to scream a lung out. I know what Ben felt because I've felt it many times myself. There was a storm cloud of its own forming in Ben's heart. He knew what was right, but it didn't matter. He knew what his heart wanted and it felt dark. The louder his flesh screamed at him the louder truth yelled back. He was faced with the dilemma of choosing.

Ben chose well and his spirit broke that day. The Stallion inside raged, but in the end sat still as better judgment rode into the arena upon his conquered foe.

"For You do not delight in sacrifice, otherwise I would give it;
You are not pleased with burnt offering.
The sacrifices of God are a broken spirit;
A broken and a contrite heart, O God, You will not despise."
- King David, *The Compass,* Psalm 51:16-17

There is nothing healthier and more life-giving than a broken spirit. We often consider brokenness as weakness and defeat, but it's the greatest victory we could ever win. As the Maker saw fit, Ben came back to camp that day without a drop of water in his tent. It turned out his rain flap was angled perfectly to prevent the rain to drift in. That night that dry bed became his rite of passage into a deeper level of manhood. He would return to his home in Nashville so much different from the person who left a couple weeks earlier.

Family...

If I were the devil I wouldn't wear red
I wouldn't have horns or a pitchfork
I wouldn't breathe fire cause it might give me away
But if I were the devil you'd never know
I'd befriend you quick and corrupt you slow
so you don't notice until it's far too late.
- Andy Gullahorn, "If I Were"[15]

God can do the supernatural. He is always changing, yet ever stays the same. In 2009, He chose to paint his picture of grace on the canvas of the family. I have never missed my wife and kids so badly in my whole life than that year in the bush. Our entire group of six had a heightened sense of longing for those we left back home.

Scott was particularly moved in the area of family. The past decade he had been leading youth groups in small to medium sized churches in north Alabama. He did so with both fruitfulness and passion. He was out several nights a week and often gone for events on the weekends. The enemy loves to sneak up on us, and he'd snuck up on Scott through his "ministry." Little by little,

Scott had allowed his priorities to take baby steps in the wrong direction. Step by step, he unknowingly began to neglect his wife and two children. Not in a dramatic way, for that is not how the enemy works. It was subtle and deceptive, and in the name of good deeds.

The time alone deep in the wilderness lulled Scott's soul into quietness enough for him to hear the deafening whisper of the Spirit in the wilderness of Alaska. Two-thirds of the way into the trip, the pent up dam of emotions and love for his family broke and the Word of God shot through Scott like the day the Maker spoke light, and it was. Scott will never be the same.

Upon his return, his actions took the place of his emotions and he made some major changes in his life. We typically imagine repentance being a single moment in time when we have an emotional experience and decide to behave differently. True repentance takes much more time than that. It is the process of re-ordering our lives toward His way instead of our way. He was determined to love his family like never before. God is so happy when we actually do something about His commands, and with Scott He was ecstatic.

To this day, four years later, Scott is still working out the details of loving his family, but his life changed that day, and as a man's life changes, so do the lives of those closest to him. God is concerned about families because the family is the visual aid for how He loves us and we are to love one another. Family is our first faith community.

The rest of the team in 2009 had similar revelations that family must be our first priority. I know I came home that year with a new vision to serve my wife and children as Redeemer serves His Body here on Earth; with love and compassion and practical acts of service. I am thankful for the stark reminder that if I can't lead my family well, I am unable to lead anyone well.

Scott Catches a Gorgeous Arctic Grayling

The Angel in Dreads

In 2010 I returned to the bush with my own group. Matt Wicks was a local church pastor in Auburn; Jonathan Del Turco started a church in Boston several years back, which had grown to the status of a healthy, growing larger church; and Bruce Donaldson had a little construction company in Pennsylvania. Peter and I were to round out the group.

When I arrived in Port Alsworth, I found out that we had another man on the journey with us. Elliot Bruce had been out the week before with Peter and another group of men led by Mark. Elliot had such a transformational experience on the trail that he committed to stay another week to help Peter with our incoming group. Elliot, the youngest at twenty-four, was a tall skinny kid with dreads and a face full of Irish red hair. I would categorize him as a hippie a few decades late. He projected an image of a rebellious twenty-something who was angry with his absent father and took it out on others by being as different as he possibly could. He was the kind of guy you would probably steer clear of if you met him on a dark street with no one else around in the middle of town. Elliot chain-smoked and drank his share of alcohol, so you can imagine that the physical exertion required by this trip was a challenge to say the least.

Jonathan Del Turco was the opposite extreme of Elliot. You would never expect to see those together anywhere, much less in the middle of the wilderness of Alaska. He was a clean-cut, conservative, law abiding, model citizen. Jonathan was the oldest of the group, actually turning fifty-seven on our trek, and probably the most intimidated by the level of challenge that lie ahead on this trip. Although he had packed and repacked his gear and worked out and prepared, he was concerned about his ability to withstand the physical pressures of this trip.

Peter was also concerned about Jonathan, but not necessarily about his readiness. Peter worried about Jonathan's ability to be transparent and vulnerable with the group. Pastors can often be protective of their image and the bush of Alaska is no place to protect your image. Peter had learned over the years that the most important thing one can do in an environment where each individual depends on all the others is to be honest. The alternative is to be what Peter called a "poser." Rule number one in the bush with Peter Goodwin was that no one was allowed to play the part of the "poser."

Jonathan and Elliot were two guys on opposite extremes; worlds apart economically, socially, generationally, in relation to values, beliefs and behaviors. The hurdle required to cross the chasm that separated the two would have seemed impossible to jump. I wondered when I met Elliot how he would survive a week with someone like Jonathan riding the heels of his chosen path. And I wondered how Jonathan would react the first time Elliot spewed out language by which Jonathan would inevitably be shocked.

*2010: Pastor Jonathan, Matt Wicks, Bruce Donaldson,
Elliot Bruce, Me and Peter*

People generalize. In other words we all have prejudices, which is part of being human. Sometimes some other less vile attitude masks our prejudice, but when the cream rises to the top, we dislike people based on our perception of others with some shared trait, role or background. We place folks in little boxes and write with a figurative black permanent marker what category they belong in. John goes in this box and I will label it "insecure." I will mark it on the top, bottom and two sides, just so I will know it when I see it. Bob goes in this other box, which I will label as "high maintenance." Jeff will fit here in the "disgruntled" box and Tom will be packaged away in "hopeless." On this side of the closet, the one closest to me, I will put Josh in the "friendly" box and Frank in the "open when needed" box.

When I was in second grade I met a boy named Johnny Wright. Johnny was a great kid... innocent and extremely shy. He was overweight and had dark skin. I lived in rural Alabama and had twelve kids in the only second grade class. They were all white and most of them were what I would consider "normal," which even in itself carries some form of prejudice.

In second grade I discovered this new emotion that I now understand to be compassion. I didn't really know what it was back then, but I knew it made me feel sad for Johnny. Johnny had no friends, only enemies. I just wanted to be Johnny's friend, not because I liked him, but because I had this new emotion that compelled me to love him.

Remember the basketball story? Well, if so, you will remember that I was not the most athletic boy in second grade. A threat from me carried about the same weight as if Pee Wee Herman said to Mike Tyson, "I'm gonna poke your eye out." I would have been voted the least likely to scare a bully in second grade.

I'm not quite sure what made those boys hate Johnny so, but it was terribly abusive how they felt about him. One day Johnny was in the boys' bathroom and three guys encircled him. Don the Bully came out of the bathroom stall and walked right over to Johnny and started to pee on him.

This newly discovered emotion that I felt started to burn and it climbed from my belly to the top of my head in a second flat. To this day I don't understand where that commanding voice came from, but it emanated from deep within. "Let him go, NOW!"

You will never believe what those boys did...they let him go.

Johnny went to the office to get a new set of clothes. I believe to this day, our principal had no idea what had happened with Johnny.

That day I learned a lesson about standing up for those who can't stand up for themselves. I became more of a man. Somehow, by the grace of the Maker, I discovered the ugliness of raw prejudice. And it moved me to a place where the passion to do something about it was greater than the fear of what would happen to me if I got my butt kicked. Now, don't get me wrong, I still fall into the dark pit of prejudice often, but I learned to know it when I see it.

Johnny Wright and I experienced a distant friendship that year. I don't know what has happened to him since.

Don and I had a couple more run-ins, but I never failed after that day to get a little respect from the bully. Maybe that is why a few years later I was invited to spend a couple of days with Don the Bully at his house. Maybe Don saw a small measure of courage in me that day in the boys' restroom that he longed for. Maybe

Don got tired of being the "poser" and hoped that he would be exposed for the little broken coward that he was. I found out during that two-day visit that Don had a tough time growing up. Not much happened as far as I could see, but who knows what the Maker did with that short visit. Then a few years later, Don was killed in a motorcycle accident at the age of twenty. I just heard it through the grapevine and didn't think much about it, but I just wonder if Don the Bully made peace with himself and with the Maker before that tragic day. Death has no prejudice—she deals every man the same hand no matter what the years leading up to her hold.

That prejudice lesson hits home to me every year as we meet the guys on each new journey through the bush. Out there, we are all the same. There are no classes that stand in the way of helping each other climb the next hill or cross the next river. There must not be; there cannot be. The next step may very well depend on it. If only I could bottle that gift up and take it home with me. If only each day and each person I met along the way could be viewed and trusted as the next means by which I survive the challenges of life. If only we thought less about our individual well-being and more about corporate well-being as we do in Alaska. What would life look like? Feel like? Be like?

There I stood looking at two opposite extremes: the hippie and the pastor. I longed to see them form a band of brothers, and I hoped that we would find the Maker together. I dream each year of a group of men walking into the bush as potential enemies and coming out with arms interlocked, changed and made new, ready to face life with a new understanding that it was the Maker who came to break down the dividing wall that makes us think one is better than the other, for it is both of us who are bound by our own vices.

When placed side by side with the Redeemer, there are no shades of darkness...only darkness and light. It is His Light that is simply reflected off of the darkness that resides deep within the soul of every man on every journey. The closer we stand, the brighter the reflection. Our only claim as light sources is how closely we choose to stand to Him. That does not make us more or less of a light source. May prejudice and pride burn away as we stand closer and closer to the true source of light.

"You are the sun shining down on everyone
Light of the world giving light to everything I see
Beauty so brilliant I can hardly take it in
And everywhere you are is warmth and light
And I am the moon with no light of my own
Still you have made me to shine
And as I glow in this cold dark night
I know I can't be a light unless I turn my face to you."
- Sara Groves, "You are the Sun"[16]

If we could scrape off the junk of life and get to the core of our being, we're all mostly the same. What we have become is simply a product of our past. It is the Maker who scrapes and shines and polishes until He gets to the brass underneath. Just like the old 1920s Emerson fan that a friend and I are restoring back home. The blades just looked like old brown aluminum blades. One day I got curious. What if we tried to polish them? What would they look like underneath? I swear to you those blades shine like stars today! It was absolutely mind boggling what lay underneath the years of residue.

Now, I'm not saying that in our heart we're all perfect. What I'm actually saying is that in our hearts we are all flawed. And what I can only hope for is that we'll all see ourselves as products of an older history; of the fallenness of that first man and woman in the garden and

187

that we'll allow the Maker to scrape and scrub and brush and polish us up with the love and redemption of the Redeemer.

Jonathan's Angel in Dreads

Jonathan and Elliot took their first step on this new journey into the wild. It took only a quarter mile or so to realize that Jonathan was not the pastor Peter had projected onto him. Jonathan was struggling, but he did not try to hide it. Each step was more difficult than the one before. A stumble here and a twisted ankle there, Jonathan was falling behind. His greatest fears were coming true. The beauty of the struggle was Jonathan's vulnerability and transparency with the group of guys. That level of openness was a breath of fresh air for Peter and later served as a healing agent that would mend up some of the brokenness in Peter's attitude toward church leaders. It was also an opportunity to see the true heart of a truly transformed man in Elliot.

As we approached our campsite from a quarter-mile away, Peter ran ahead to scope the landscape and I traveled a hundred or so yards in front of the pack. Jonathan and Elliot took up the rear. I stopped and waited. I listened intently for some noise to know the guys behind us were okay. Nothing. I waited some more. Nothing. A few minutes later, I could hear a rustling in the distance and some men talking. I watched as, once again, a beautiful portrait of redemption broke through the tree line.

I reflected as I saw Elliot, the displaced hippie, leading Jonathan, the conservative pastor, in the same parade of grace that I saw on the other side of this mountain two years earlier. Elliot was sporting two large backpacks, one in front and the other behind, as

Jonathan, the conservative pastor, trailed behind laughing and smiling just as Mark had been before. Once again I was in awe of the work of the Maker in the life of these two polar opposite pilgrims on this journey of grace.

From that point on, Jonathan referred to Elliot as his "angel in dreads." Jonathan swears that he would not have made it to camp that day had his angel in dreads not rescued him.

What were the chances? What were the odds that these two opposites would so quickly discover that they were not as different as they thought? It must have been a healing moment for both the hippie and the pastor as they traveled through their own wormholes that day.

Drop your guard. Be interdependent. Walk the journey that can only be walked hand in hand with others one step at a time. Realize that we are all simply products of our past and that with the help of Redeemer we can be polished into everything that He meant us to be.

Jonathon's Angel in Dreads with the Catch of the Day

The Ridge Runners

Two days into our 2010 trek, Matt Wicks had talked Peter into a hike into the mountains. Peter had planned an aggressive trip to both challenge and amaze us. We expected to be hiking the ridge of the mountains for about four to six hours. Jonathan and Bruce paddled us across the lake to our starting point and dropped Peter, Elliot, Matt and me. We would take a ridge to the top and hike across the ridge of the mountains, drop down on the other side near the camp and have a hearty dinner together around the campfire.

As we made our way up the ridge a thick fog dropped in on us. It was the kind of fog you can taste. We were engulfed with a cloud. I was hurting! I had not had a chance to work out as much as I had in the previous years and I was not up for the physical challenge that this hike required. We had taken one meal of dehydrated food each and one burner to cook it with. We each had a supply of water and Peter was carrying extra in his pack. As we made it to the top, the fog continued to rest below us. It looked as if it had settled in for the day.

As we began to cross the ridge, we realized that it wasn't as flat as we thought across the top. A couple of times we would have to drop eight hundred feet down a gravel wall just to take a thousand-foot climb up the other side. After three or four hours, I was done. I felt like I couldn't take another step. We stopped at the bottom of one of those eight-hundred-foot drops and found a fresh water supply. We refilled our water bags and sat and rested for a time. Then we started back up the rock wall on the other side.

That was the hardest climb in all my Alaskan experiences. We would reach what we thought to be a peak and turn a corner just to find another one. After a few of those, we made it to our highest point, although we didn't know it at the time. Then we started a horizontal hike across a relatively flat trail, which obviously served lots of bear, moose and wolf, as it was well-worn. The skinny foot trail turned into two parallel trails as we moved along. This was where the big bear traveled, with the two trails representing right feet and left feet.

As we continued on that trail I heard some yelping sounds. Peter stopped and said, "Listen to those wolf cubs."

I was concerned, but Peter reminded us that wolves generally steer clear of people and other animals, so there was no danger.

In a meadow on the side of one of those steep peaks, we stopped and fell to the ground exhausted. I reached down and started devouring one of my favorite wild treats in the Alaskan Wilderness; fresh blueberries.

The Maker knows exactly what we need and this break from the climb up the mountain was perfect. I love to pop the berries in between my teeth and apply just enough pressure for them to shoot the juice out and saturate my mouth. The blueberry stops seem to provide just the energy and motivation I need to jump up and take the next section of the mountain with the anticipation of what is over that next peak.

It's funny: the blueberry meadows are always in a clearing, so the view is usually spectacular. It's like a busy day at work when I feel like I don't have the will to carry on. When the day is done and I make my way home to see my family, I walk in the front door and have a "blueberry" moment.

We painted our front door a couple of years ago, and the paint on the door sticks to the paint on the frame. When the door opens, it makes this loud ripping sound as the two paints tear apart. It can be heard throughout the house, so all the kids know when daddy is home. "Hi dada," my youngest yells when she hears the front door open. Then Daniel comes running to get his first glimpse of daddy for the night. I make my way around the house giving hugs and kisses to the rest of the family. It's a beautiful sight and a much-needed reminder that someday we'll forget all the struggles and all the pain and what will remain is the beauty of blueberries and children.

Then the weather changed—cold wind blew in. We all pulled jackets out of our bags and put them on. On the ground we had been enjoying sixty-five and seventy-degree weather. How could it be so cold up here? A few minutes later a super fine mist began to moisten the right side of our faces. It was as fine a mist as I had ever felt. The right side of my face got colder. Peter was in the front; I was following closely behind and Matt and Elliot were twenty feet behind. I looked back and the left sides of their faces were white while the right sides were beet red.

We came to a plateau on the top of the mountain and Peter stopped and looked around as if trying to get his bearings. It became clear that Peter was confused about our location. Over the next couple of hours, the reality hit me that we were in for a long day!

Everyone, except for Peter, who seemed utterly confident until the end, wondered what we should do next. We could hunker down where we were and wait it out until morning. The problem with that was that the guys on the ground would be freaked out about what to do. Our other option was to keep on moving. So we did.

I wondered if Peter was really as confident as he seemed. I wondered if, in his head, he was really as afraid as I. It's dangerous to doubt your leader; it causes your mind to swim around in a future filled with all sorts of monsters. Fear conjures up visions from the very pit of hell when you think you're all alone. That's what's so great about following the Maker; He knows what was, what is, and what will be. Our job is just to stay in step, look straight ahead and follow His lead. When we stray away from that, like the New Testament hero Peter, who took his eyes off Redeemer as he was skimming across the top of that lake two thousand years ago, we begin to sink down into the fears that consume us.

The game with my mind was on again. I wondered if I would ever return to my place of comfort and safety. I wondered if I would ever see my kids again, or hug my wife. This place seemed so massive and I...we seemed so small.

We were no matches for the likes of the wilderness of Alaska! It felt like we were helpless. Of course, my mind was exaggerating reality. I was with an experienced guide and we were relatively close to help. That's what happens when we escape our comfort zones: our minds tell us powerful half-truths and the half-truths sound so much like reality, until the wake of damage they leave behind reveals that half-truths are worse than whole-lies.

When I feel totally out of control, my natural response is to blame someone. I began to search in my mind for the perfect person: I was angry with Peter. Of course, it could be his fault. I had had it with myself, too, but the excuses come easy when I'm trying to blame myself, so that didn't last very long. And once again, I found myself ticked off with God.

When I realized that I was helpless in the wilderness, I re-visited the feelings of before "Our Place" and basked in the remembrance of how it felt to be taken advantage of. That's what I felt God had done, taken advantage of my innocent excitement of the wilderness. The one thing I thought would help me find a new peace in my life had been the one thing that had led me to a place of danger.

I remember feeling this sense of anger and lack of control once before. When I was only sixteen years old, there was a man in my life that I viewed as my hero. He was my safety net and had been my rescuer when I would make stupid decisions and behave irresponsibly. We would hang out on occasion. One night he lost his temper and crossed the forbidden land into a fit of rage. He physically beat someone up that night right in front of me and I was crushed under the weight of the unimaginable. My hero had not only made a terrible mistake, but he crossed over the line of inhumanity. I lived the vulnerable life of a child under the safe wings of just a few people and the one who I trusted most, suddenly became dangerous. How does one process that so quickly? What affect does that radical shift in the paradigm of life have on a young man?

I was angry and I blamed the man. The reality was that he was simply a product of his past, a carrier of the pain and confusion that caused this type of rage to spill over his boundaries of reason and self-control. None of that mattered that night. I became immediately aware of my lack of safety and security and the world seemed so large. As large as that wilderness that we were roaming around in on that cold, wet day in Alaska.

God loves to find us wandering outside our safety zone. He basks in reminding us that we really are out of control and unsafe without his embrace. He is the redeemer of these times and He was about the business of redeeming the days following my transition from safety to insecurity that dark day at the age of sixteen. I had just been introduced to the Maker a few weeks earlier and He wanted to redeem the tragedy of that night of violence into a visual aid that would teach me to cling to Him and Him alone. And that I did!

We learn slowly and forget quickly. That day on the mountain I forgot that the Maker was there with us—I felt alone and vulnerable. Yet, if we had died out there in the wilderness, it would have just been a transition from now to eternity. Death is not really as big a deal as we make it. He is the God of life and of death, He is the God of now and forever, and we are His precious children.

I was angry with Peter because I just wanted to start going down. If we had gotten to this place by going up couldn't we just go down and return? Peter said that if we headed straight down we would most certainly get stuck in a ravine too deep to cross and too wide to jump. I trusted him, but I did so kicking and screaming in my mind. I reasoned that he probably knew best since he had spent so much time out there. But that didn't stop my angry restless mind from fighting.

About ten hours into the hike, we stopped to try once again to get our bearings. Peter looked back at me and the other two and said, "Well, fellas, you got any ideas?"

I knew we were in trouble before that moment, but that took it over the top.

Matt piped up and said, "Yeah, let's pray."

196

Matt is one of those guys that would be smiling if his dog were dying. His positive attitude is infectious as he finds a way to laugh about almost anything. Although the corners of his mouth still arched upward in a peaceful smile, his voice was a little more serious this time. So we prayed.

As we finished our prayer and looked up across a valley in front of us, the fog dissipated for only a moment, and we had a chance to get our bearings. We were all blown away by the grace of God in that moment. Our last resort of talking to Redeemer was the tool we needed to dig our way out of this mess we were in. That brief moment of clear views gave us just what we needed to get back on track toward camp.

We were still a couple of hours in the woods trying to backtrack as we realized we had overshot our mark by about a half-mile; it sounds so insignificant as I write this story in the comfort of my favorite little coffee shop, but out in the wild a half-mile feels like the difference between life and death.

When we neared camp late that night, I was in the most pain I had ever felt. I could hardly make the last few steps to enter into our camp, which felt like the safest place on Earth. Just a day ago, that same place felt dangerous and vulnerable, now it felt like the underground bunker of the White House. I could not have been happier to see the tops of those brightly colored tents flapping in the Alaskan wind on the shores of Lake Kijik.

As I was entering into camp I was given one of the greatest gifts of my life. I looked up from my painful ascent toward safety and saw conservative pastor Jonathan waving his hands through the air, shouting praises to the Maker and jumping for joy waving us home as if we were arriving back from overseas after a long-fought battle for freedom. As I got nearer I realized that he was shedding tears of joy over our return "home."

How could it be?

I had thought before this that his concern for these few guys he had never met must be exaggerated. I was sure he couldn't possibly care for us as much as he put on. I had a measure of disdain in my arrogant heart for the way he seemed so interested in us when he talked. And I felt certain that his image was what he was most concerned about. But not anymore! Those tears were the real deal. Those drops of water gliding down his cheeks were sent to soften the fallow ground of my soul and the moistened ground was able to receive a seed of love. That seed sprouted and its fruit forced me to embrace the idea that man really can extend the love of the Maker in all its power toward another human being.

I am thankful that the Maker loves us just as we are, but also loves us enough to not let us stay that way. Pastor Jonathon's love for us was simply the voice of God whispering in my ear, "I care so deeply about you. You cannot run from my love."

Pastor Jonathon Having the Time of His Life!

My Next Adventure

"The glory of God is man fully alive; moreover man's life is the vision of God: if God's revelation through creation has already obtained life for all the beings that dwell on earth, how much more will the Word's manifestation of the Father obtain life for those who see God." - St. Irenaeus

"What's lost is nothing to what's found, and all the death that ever was, set next to life, would scarcely fill a cup."
- Frederick Buechner in <u>Godric</u>[17]

So here I am...on July 28th, 2012, sitting on Delta Flight 2207 headed for Seattle and then onward to Alaska once again.

The flight is familiar; the feelings not so much. I have been more emotional the past few days than I expected. Usually the busyness of the preparation drowns out the nagging voice of fear, doubt and loneliness that accompanies a trip like this, but for some reason I just wanted to say goodbye to those who have meant so much to me this year. And so I did. I spent the whole day yesterday visiting, emailing and calling those in my circle of life. Why has it been more poignant this year?

I think I sensed an urgency to say goodbye to what was. I've never been to Alaska without returning a new man...a different person down deep. Along with that different person comes a difference in relationships. I know that when I return, the foundation upon which those relationships were built will be tweaked a bit. The Maker will bring a new clarity into my life...a new *modus operandi*. When our perspective changes, it changes the way we live our life on a day-to-day basis, and that changes how we invest and receive from those closest to us.

As I sit here writing this passage I wonder what I will be saying goodbye to on this sixth trip to the place where it all started.

Bruce, Peter and I, have taken the trip before. Nathan works with me in my little furniture consignment shop in Auburn; Marty is an accountant who I know from the store and Austin is his son, a senior in high school. It is a rag-tag team and I look forward to what we will experience together as we go headlong into the bush of Alaska.

The 2012 Original Design Adventure Team

This morning I bid farewell to my wife and four children. They love their daddy...and he loves them. Julie has been such a trooper through these adventures. What more could a man ask for than a woman who will stand behind him even when his decisions make her life more complicated? My absence will most certainly create a hole in the day-to-day functioning of our family. But she sees in me a dream; a passion to take men to the place where everything changed for me and to share it. Her desire to see me live to the fullest is greater than her desire to make life easy. She is more than I deserve.

It's been a tough couple of years. Life has dished out more than I felt like I could take at times. I have worked as hard as ever and the day-to-day grind has sucked life right out of my soul. I am so tired. In times like these, adventure is not as appealing as it should be.

A few weeks ago I read a book. I read it in a day...that never happens. I just couldn't put it down. I lay on the couch all day devouring what would become a life-changing piece of literature for me. In *A Thousand Miles in a Million Years*, Donald Miller went on and on about living a better story. He talked about choosing to put oneself in a position to invite adventure into life and then to step through every door of opportunity as it presented itself. I listened intently.

As I lie on the couch and read those words, the Maker began to speak to my heart again. The heart that had been so tired for so long; the heart that could hardly hear anymore through the screaming voices of urgency that wouldn't leave me alone from day to day. And when that heart heard the voice of truth ring louder, it began to pump harder.

"Dream," it was screaming. "By God, dream again! Let the darkness of failure and despair be swallowed up like death in the grave by the power of Life."

For, as Frederick Buechner says, "What's lost is nothing to what's found, and all the death that ever was, set next to life, would scarcely fill a cup."[18]

I dreamt of life together with people who would live each day like we were dying. A group of people who could put the doubts to rest and dig deep for a life that is more than we currently have.

And I dreamt about Alaska again. A part of me belongs there. It is not the place that saves me, but the work of the Maker in that place. He chose that place to invite me into a better story and I accepted the invitation. And as Miller says in his book, "Once you know what it takes to live a better story, you don't have a choice. Not living a better story would be like deciding to die, deciding to walk around numb until you die, and it's not natural to want to die."[19]

I long to see my kids running in the wildflowers there. I long to stand on the peak of a mountain with my wife by my side. I long to sit around a campfire and sing songs to the Maker with those closest to me.

The other day I was sitting in a forest back home. As I reflected, I felt the Maker begin to speak to me. As He whispered in my ear, I began to breathe deeply and felt new life flood into my veins. "It is not over," He said, "it has only just begun." I was writing a note to Julie when I heard it most clearly. "It is not over, it has just begun."

What was He talking about? I'm sure I still do not completely know. But, the best I can figure, He was talking about adventure. The experience of stepping out to do the things that most people shy away from is the beginning of adventure. The gypsies experienced it on the first trip in 1996; Julie and I stepped out in the first two years of our life together; Peter and I experienced it on our first journey deep into the bush. There I sat, looking at the water clapping its hands as it ran over the rocks of that riverbed, as God said, "It's not over, it has only just begun."

As I continued to reflect on that statement, I thought about my life over the past few years. I have begun to let adventure wane. We have four children now, we run a business that requires our presence, we are not as young as we once were—shouldn't we be slowing down the pace of adventure in our lives?

And then I thought about my children. I have such a deep longing for them to live a better story. What could I do for them that would make their lives worth the living? What better gift could I give them than adventure? The most exciting and fulfilling adventure is that of recklessly abandoning to the ways of the Maker.

He is so creative. He longs for us to live our lives in abandon to His ways. He promises to provide for us like He does for the birds of the air. He promises to clothe us like the flowers of the field, and He promises that our life will be abundantly full of His life; and His life is full of adventure.

I am reminded of the words from John Eldredge in his book, "Sacred Romance"…"One of the most poisonous of all Satan's whispers is simply, 'Things will never change.' That lie kills expectation, trapping our heart forever in the present. To keep desire alive and flourishing, we must renew our vision for what lies ahead. Things will not always be like this. Jesus has promised to "make all things new." Eye has not seen, ear has not heard all that God has in store for his lovers, which does not mean 'we have no clue so don't even try to imagine,' but rather, you cannot outdream God." [20]

I have seen it so often. It seems the Maker sometimes waits for us to take the first step of abandon. Then He frees us from what may have held us back.

If nothing made that first step seem impossible, would it be a step of faith at all?

I can't help but wonder what the future will hold, only time will tell. That part is up to the Maker. What I do know is that He loves me enough to poke me again and make me dream.

"What ifs" are the doorways into new adventures. "Why nots" are the doorknobs. We turn knobs and tug at doors until we find the one that opens for us. The Maker will leave that one unlocked and when we get to the other side, the light will be on and He'll be waiting with all the resources and help we need to fulfill His best desires for us.

What about you? What is your next step? To what is the beckoning voice of the Maker calling? Cling tightly to your "what ifs" and "why nots." They are precious treasures if you long to live the life of adventure with the Maker.

Your story will probably not even remotely resemble mine. These stories are just a small fraction of all the adventure that God has had or will have for my family.

My motivation is not to impress you with my faith or experiences; it is to prod you to recklessly abandon to the beckoning call of the Maker.

You will face obstacles and often it will seem impossible. But take heart…all that's required of you are a few "what ifs" and "why nots." Swing wide the door and enter into the life of adventure that God has uniquely designed for you.

You will never regret it!

The Conclusion Up to Now

"THE TEMPTATION is always to reduce life to size. A bowl of cherries. A rat race. Amino acids. Even to call it a mystery smacks of reductionism. It is the mystery." - Frederick Buechner in Wishful Thinking[21]

My first trip to Alaska was not the beginning of the stories; it was simply the gateway into the rest. I cannot even begin to explain how that first journey has affected every aspect of my life since we set out in the ARK02 with the three gypsies. I moved to Florida, finished Bible college, helped plant a church in Colorado, chose my wife, tweaked my life goals, developed a philosophy of child rearing, spent thousands of dollars sharing Alaska with other men and dove deeply into the practice of making disciples who make disciples.

But these stories are not stories of my experiences in Alaska—they are stories of the Maker's redemption of the brokenness in my life and His faithfulness to lead me to a life worth living. They are stories of me trading a few conveniences and successes that life has to offer for the adventure and richness that Life has to offer.

A few months ago, we had a picture hanging in our living room that read: "It costs nothing to dream and everything not to." I loved that picture. One night I was sitting in my man-chair thinking about it when I decided that it was a lie. It costs everything to dream. If you pursue what you feel compelled to do with your life, it will cost everything.

In my mind I imagine a hot dog vendor walking through a crowded baseball stadium with a promise of a hot frankfurter in exchange for a sacrifice of a couple dollars. The voice triggers a hunger that compels me to indulge in the greasy dog. Much the same way, the Maker is crying out that there is more; more to life than this. It does, however, come at a price. The price is our life. Will we give our motivation to the fullness He promises? Will we hand over our plans in exchange for His? It is the one indulgence that makes Him happy and sets our hearts free. It is the one addiction that all other addictions impersonate. It is the vice to which we were meant to submit. What more can we expect from life than these experiences that the Maker had planned from the beginning of time? Let go and fall headlong into the future that the Maker has designed specifically and uniquely for YOU. You will not turn back!

As I blindly followed Scott into obedience and journeyed north, I simply heard the beckoning call of the Maker in a particular place, and that place has become a Stone of Remembrance for me.

When the Israelites crossed into the Maker's Promised Land, Joshua instructed them to construct pillars that would help future generations remember the faithfulness of God. Parents, grandparents and great-grandparents would stand beside those stones and tell about the faithfulness of the Maker and how He delivered them from danger and defeat, even the danger that they were to themselves, for they longed to return to captivity at times instead of facing the challenge before them.